INTRODUCING
THE BIBLE

Introducing the Bible

Gerald Hughes and Stephen Travis

A LION BOOK

Published by
Lion Publishing
Icknield Way, Tring, Herts, England
ISBN 0 85648 162 9
Albatross Books
PO Box 320, Sutherland, NSW 2232, Australia
ISBN 0 86760 237 6

Editorial and additional material
Jean Morgan
Derek Williams

Illustrations
Evelyn Bartlett: pp. 9, 16, 17
Vic Mitchell: pp. 67, 100, 104, 105
David Reddick: pp. 21, 43, 79
Edward Ripley: pp. 68, 69, 94, 95, 96, 110, 121, 122,
124
Ray Wright: pp. 88, 89

Maps
Roy Lawrance and Lesley Passey

First edition 1981

Printed in Italy by New Interlitho S.P.A., Milan

The photographs in this book are reproduced by
permission of the following photographers and
organizations:
J. C. Allen: 61, 106, 117
British Museum: 10 (all), 11, 14, 25 (below), 26, 50,
51 (all)
Camera Press: 3, 74, 96
Elisabeth Photo Library: 22 (right), 118
Sonia Halliday Photographs: F. H. C. Birch 28, 58, 86,
120; Sonia Halliday 2, 4, 7, 19, 25 (above), 27, 30, 32,
33, 39 (left), 42, 47, 65, 71, 73, 80, 83, 84, 102, 119,
127; Jane Taylor 8, 20, 39 (right), 54, 107, 108, 111,
112, 114
Lion Publishing, David Alexander: 1, 48, 56
Mansell Collection: 94, 95, 123 (both)
Ann and Bury Peerless: 13
Claire Schwob: 63
Ronald Sheridan: 15, 77, 93
Stephen Travis: 22 (left), 35, 53, 72, 75, 91, 97, 101,
103, 110

Contents

THE BIRTH OF A NATION 1
The dawn of history 2
The human difference 2
Other accounts of creation 3
Man goes it alone 4
Other accounts of the flood 4
From herdsmen to slaves 6
Abram's journeys 6
Problems of faith 7
Sumer: cradle of civilization 10
Joseph the dreamer 11
The shepherd-kings of Egypt 12
Escape to freedom 13
Slaves in Egypt 13
Birth of a leader 14
The exodus 18
Journey's end 19
The covenant 20
Settling in Canaan 22
A new leader 22
Conquest 24
Sea-borne invaders 25
A Canaanite city 26
Food laws and animal sacrifices 27
Problems of unity 29
Who were the judges? 31
The story of Ruth 31

**THE GROWTH OF THE
KINGDOM 33**
The kingdom established 34
Samuel the prophet 35
Israel's first king 36
Saul's downfall 37
Saul and David 38
Hero and outlaw 38
The kingdom united 40
Government and religion under King David 40
Solomon: builder and merchant 41
Solomon's temple 43
The kingdom divided 45
A fatal decision 45
Prophets and politics 48
Elijah denounces idolatry 48
The Assyrians 50
Threats from Assyria 52
Amos and social justice 53
Who were the prophets? 54
Peace in Judah 55
Hezekiah and the Assyrians 56
The Book of Isaiah 57
Josiah's reforms 59
The teaching of Jeremiah 61
Questions of life and death 62

THE END OF AN ERA   65
The end of the exile   66
Rebuilding in Judah   67
Babylon: city of promise   67
The Persians   68
Ezra teaches the law   70
The Aramaic language   70
Nehemiah rebuilds the walls   71
Jerusalem   72
The Samaritans   74
The development of Jewish religion   75
Pharisees   75
Jewish festivals   76
Sadducees   78
Essenes   78
The hope for a messiah   78
How the Old Testament was compiled   80
An outline of the Old Testament story   81
Visions of the future   84
Between the testaments   86
The rise of Greece   86
Judah under the Ptolemies   87
Judah under the Greeks   90
The Maccabaean Revolt   90
The conquest of Galilee   92
The Roman influence   92
The Jewish 'Dispersion'   93
The Jews and Rome   94

THE BIRTH OF CHRISTIANITY   97
Jesus and his world   99
Jesus' birth   99
Jesus in Nazareth   100
Jesus the teacher in Galilee   101
Journeys of Jesus   103
Working life in Palestine   104
The road to Jerusalem   107
The synagogue   108
The resurrection   109
The tomb of Jesus   110
Josephus, historian of the Jews   111
Taxation in Judea   112
The first Christians   113
The church is born   113
The church begins to grow   114
Jews and Christians   115
Paul the traveller   116
Saul of Tarsus   116
The first journey, AD 46–47   117
The second journey, AD 50–52   119
Religions of the Roman Empire   122
The third journey, AD 52–56   124
The man and his methods   125
Jerusalem to Rome, AD 60–61   126
The seven churches of Asia   127
How the New Testament was compiled   128

Preface

The Bible is probably the world's best-known book; it is certainly the world's best-seller. Some of its major characters – Moses and Jesus, for instance – have become twentieth-century heroes of stage and screen. The poignant story of the Good Samaritan, and Jesus' deceptively demanding 'golden rule' of doing to others what we would have them do to us, have each contributed to popular ideals of morality.

Above all, Christians throughout the world have based their beliefs and behaviour on its teachings. And the Jews continue to use and revere two-thirds of it, the Old Testament.

Despite its popularity, however, large portions of the Bible remain literally a closed book to many people. The reason is not hard to find. The Bible is not a continuous narrative with a handful of main characters acting out a straightforward plot. It is a collection of sixty-six different books, each with its own theme and literary style. Some are largely poetry and others theology. There are books of history: accounts of battles and the exploits of kings. Visions, stories and moral advice also find an important place within the Bible.

The people whose names and deeds are recorded in its pages are not very different from people of any age. But the age they lived in *was* different: the customs and culture which form the backcloth to the events seem totally alien to the experience of many modern readers.

The world of the Bible was a pre-technological society of slow travel and laborious work, a pastoral environment of small farms and cottage industry. The images the Bible writers chose to represent and describe their insights about God and the always-burning issues of life and death came directly from the cornfields and battlefields of the Near East centuries ago.

It is the purpose of this book to chart that background. It sets the biblical events in their historical, cultural and geographical context. Some help is also given to enable the reader to unravel the cultural strings that tie together the message and meaning of the Bible. For the genius of the Bible is in its timeless theme of God's dealings with human beings. The theme becomes more relevant, not less, as the background is unveiled.

Some regard the Bible merely as a record of a former age, interesting but unrelated to contemporary life. Others treat it as a book of proof-texts, the context being largely incidental. This book tries to avoid both extremes. If we can recapture the attitudes and life-styles of the times we will be that much closer to understanding the intention and meaning of the writers.

THE BIRTH OF A NATION

Since the dawn of history, the fortunes of individual nations have ebbed and flowed like the ocean tides. Some, at the short-lived height of their power, have made their mark on the world and then drifted into obscurity, if not extinction.

The Old Testament records almost 2,000 turbulent years in the history of a small but significant group of people in the Near East – Israel. During that time they grew from a wandering tribe into an established nation. They were attacked and harassed by many ruling powers, but the Jewish culture and religion outlived them all, and still exists today.

However, this story is not simply one of survival, nor does it ignore the short-comings and failings of Israel itself. Rather, it is the story of how, through crises, defeats, and occasional prosperity, the first Jews discovered something of the character and purpose of God.

The dawn of history

The title of Genesis, the first book in the Bible, means 'beginning'. Its timeless opening chapters are the story of the creation of the world, and in particular, the story of man's beginnings on the earth and the relationship he has with his creator.

The Bible assumes the reality of God from the outset and no attempt is made to explain or argue for his existence. He is the God of light and darkness, the heavens and the earth, summer and winter. Everything owes its origin to the creator and everything that he made is good.

The forming of man is seen as the supreme creative act of God. It is man's relationship with God that provides the main theme of the rest of Genesis and indeed of the whole of the Bible.

The human difference

Genesis 2:7

The two opening chapters of Genesis build up a picture of the world as God first made it. People, says the writer, are made from the materials that are to be found in the earth. God's living breath, or 'spirit', acts upon the lifeless physical matter and gives it life: for according to the Hebrew mind, all life is

In the Genesis account of creation, God put man in charge of the animal kingdom. Here, a Turkish shepherd in Cyprus holds the prize ram from his flock.

Other accounts of creation

	GENESIS	ATRAHASIS (An early Babylonian story)	BABYLONIAN CREATION STORY
Genesis does not contain the only account of creation which circulated in the ancient world. Many civilizations attempted to explain the origins of the earth and its people. But only Genesis speaks of a single, supreme God, who creates mankind to share in the good things he has made.	God alone exists.	The gods and the world already exist.	Two Oceans exist: Tiamat and Apsu. Other gods, their children, also exist.
	At first all was waste.	Minor gods are working to irrigate the land.	
	God creates light, the heavens, dry land with greenery.		Tiamat is angry at the noisy and hilarious behaviour of her children. Apsu decides to destroy his noisy offspring, but is himself killed by Ea god of water and wisdom. Tiamat, under pressure from a group of rebel gods, decides to avenge Apsu's death.
	The sun, moon and stars become visible.	The hard work makes the gods angry and they rebel.	
	Fish are made to live in the waters and birds to fly in the heavens.		Tiamat breeds a horde of monsters and sends them, under the leadership of Kingu, to wreak vengeance on the gods, who retaliate and are repulsed. Marduk the son of Ea offers to act as a champion of the gods if they make him their king.
	Animals are made to live on the dry land.		
			Marduk kills Tiamat, slits her body in two like a fish. Of one half he makes the earth and of the other the sky.
			All gods, including the rebels, accept the authority of Marduk. Kingu is arrested and killed.
	God makes man of the same stuff as animals, but with a different nature, being in God's image.	Man is made of the flesh and blood of the rebel leader mixed with clay.	Man is made from the blood of Kingu.
		Man takes over the hard work of the gods.	Man is set to work on the earth to provide food and drink for the gods.
	God rests.	The gods relax.	The gods relax and Marduk is given Babylon as his city.

the property of God. Neither spirit nor matter disappears, but their coming together has created something new. This animated matter is called 'a living being' or soul. Man is a unity, a 'body-spirit'.

Despite this emphasis, some people have thought of man as if he were a 'spiritual being' whose body and mind are of less importance than his soul. This is not a picture that the Bible writers give: it is a Greek idea. What the Hebrews meant by 'soul' is roughly equivalent to the English word 'personality'.

Genesis 1:20,24,30

In fact, the Bible uses the term 'living being' not only of a person, but also of the animals. People and the animals are all 'living beings' or 'living creatures' – the words are the same in Hebrew. So the use of the word 'soul' is not intended to distinguish man from the animals. But despite the similarities,

Genesis insists that there is still something special about man.

Genesis 1:26,27 God, it says, made man in his own image. At first sight it may seem as if the writer imagined God to have a physical shape that man somehow *resembles*. But wherever the Hebrew word 'image' is used in other passages in the Old Testament, outside Genesis, it refers to an object that *represents* a god. People are God's representatives in the world and the 'image' mentioned in Genesis is shown by the way they live. Their task is to demonstrate God's care and concern for people and the rest of the creation.

Man goes it alone

To fulfil this task, man needs to remain in close relationship with God. Genesis, however, presents a picture of the human decision to break that relationship, to become self-sufficient, and to live without reference to God. This story is told in a poetic and dramatic form where Adam and Eve eat the forbidden fruit. Man chose his own way, to become like a god rather than remain obedient to God.

Genesis 3

The result of this rebellion against God was that man was

Other accounts of the flood

The major cultures of the ancient Near East also had their own flood stories. In all three, man's behaviour prompts the divine action, in Genesis because man has become wicked, in the others because he is too noisy.

GENESIS

Man rebels against God and is expelled from the garden.

Man begins to increase and build cities. But his behaviour disturbs God. To punish man's sin God decides to send a flood to destroy his creation, but warns the loyal Noah to build a large ark, or floating box, and take his family and representatives of the animal kingdom on board for safety.

When the floods quieten, Noah's boat comes to rest on a high mountain.

After forty days, Noah sends out a raven, but it finds no place to rest so returns to the ark. After a further seven days, Noah sends out a dove and this action is repeated again twice before the bird ceases to return.

Noah then leaves the ark and offers a burnt sacrifice to God who promises not to destroy the world again by flood and gives the rainbow as a sign of his promise.

ATRAHASIS (Babylonian)

No record of man's rebellion against the gods.

Mankind begins to increase. The noise of man disturbs the gods who send plagues, famines and droughts hoping that man will take the hint and make less noise.

A conference of the gods is called and the decision is reached to destroy mankind entirely.

Enki, the creator, tells his favourite, Atrahasis, of the plot to destroy man by a flood. Atrahasis escapes with his family and some animals in a great boat.

When the flood ends Atrahasis offers a sacrifice and the gods gather round the smoke eager for their food.

Most of them promise never to cause such destruction again. The god whose sleep was disturbed is not entirely appeased, however.

GILGAMESH EPIC (Assyrian)

Man has increased in numbers and his noise disturbs the gods. Enlil the god of power and Ishtar the goddess of fertility encourage the other gods to destroy mankind.

Ea, the god of water and wisdom, warns his favourite man Utnapishtim to build a boat when the flood comes. The man, his family and the animals enter the boat.

The gods are terrified by the flood and flee to the highest heaven.

After seven days the storm subsides and the boat runs aground on a mountain. After another seven days Utnapishtim sends out a dove and later a swallow. Both return. Then a raven is sent who does not return.

Utnapishtim opens the boat and on the mountain top he makes a sacrifice over which the gods gather like flies. The gods promise never to destroy again and Utnapishtim and his wife are made immortal.

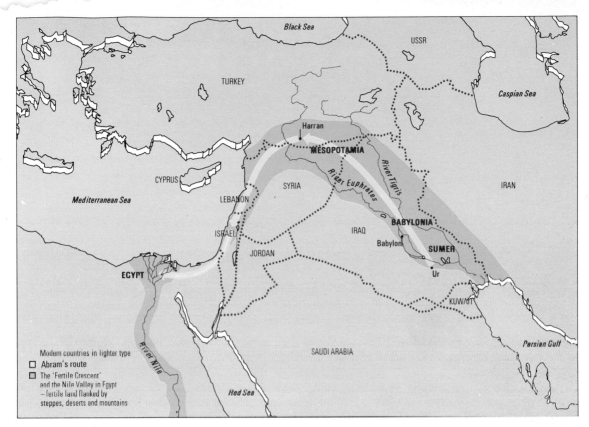

Abram's journeys

Modern countries in lighter type
☐ Abram's route
☐ The 'Fertile Crescent'
and the Nile Valley in Egypt
– fertile land flanked by
steppes, deserts and mountains

Genesis 6–9
Genesis 11:1-9

expelled from the garden where he had lived in close contact with God. But the story goes on to illustrate the strong Hebrew emphasis on the mercy of God. Although God drives the man and woman from the garden, he does not destroy them.

This theme is developed both in the story of the flood and in the story of the Tower of Babel. Man had turned from God and become a rebel; God had expelled him from his perfect surroundings. Yet it appears that this action did not deal with the problem; for man continued to rebel. Again and again, God punished him, but on every occasion hope remained. The flood did not destroy everyone; for Noah, his family and representatives of the animal kingdom were saved. Later on, men were dispersed from Babel, yet not wiped out. There remained hope for the future.

The opening eleven chapters of Genesis provide an introduction or, better still, a prologue, to the dramatic message of the Bible. The whole world is God's creation. Man is intended to be God's representative in creation, but man's rebellion has led to serious consequences and no matter how often the judgement of God falls, the problem of human sinfulness remains. So, at the end of Genesis 11, there hangs a question mark. What is God going to do with his rebel creature? The way God tackles this problem is the subject of the remainder of the Bible.

From herdsmen to slaves

The Old Testament story of the Jewish nation – and hence the story of Christianity – begins with a wandering herdsman called Abram. He lived in Ur, a prosperous city near the mouth of the River Euphrates. After the death of his brother he left the city with Terah his father, Sarai his wife, and his nephew Lot.

Genesis 11:31 They planned to travel west to Canaan, near the Mediterranean, but settled for a while in Harran, in northern Mesopotamia. Like Ur, it was the centre of worship of the moon god Sin.

Abram's family were not the only ones moving across the rich land known as the Fertile Crescent about 1900 BC. Many tribes were changing their territories and looking for new places to settle in. Abram was travelling with herds of animals and during his journeys would have lived in tents similar to those used by modern Bedouin arabs. Although the camel was in use during this period, it did not become a major means of transport until the time of Solomon, nearly 1,000 years later.

Abram's journeys

People had first begun to live in cities before 4500 BC in Mesopotamia, a land which lay between the rivers Tigris and Euphrates, in modern-day Iraq. The cities were often self-governing districts (city-states) rather than large towns. The two most important peoples were the Sumerians and the Semites. The origins of the Sumerians are uncertain, but the Semites take their name from Shem, one of Noah's sons. They were the ancestors of a number of races including the Jews.

The city-states of Mesopotamia remained independent until about 2400 BC. Then the Semites, under their king Sargon I, took control of the whole region. But when Sargon died in 2316 BC Mesopotamia entered a period of unrest which lasted for more than a century. Eventually the Sumerians won back control and Mesopotamia became peaceful and prosperous, although it was frequently attacked by neighbouring peoples. Suddenly, about 2000 BC, the great Sumerian Empire fell apart and the land once more came under Semitic rule.

In the Semitic culture of this period people laid great stress on the need for married couples to have children who would carry on the family name. But Abram and Sarai were childless, bitterly disappointed that they had no heir.

In such a situation they could adopt a servant and name him as their heir. Alternatively, Sarai could give Abram one of her female servants as a substitute wife. Any resulting children

Abram and his family lived in tents similar to those still used by modern Bedouin nomads.

could continue the family line. And although Abram would appear to have two wives, only Sarai would have any legal rights as a wife.

Letters and inscriptions have been discovered at Nuzi in north-east Mesopotamia which show that these customs were common among the people of the Fertile Crescent about this time. Discoveries such as these have gone a long way to show that the stories of Abram, Isaac, and Jacob fit into the Middle Bronze Age period – that is between 2000 and 1550 BC.

The Bible says little about the many tribes travelling at the same time as Abram. The Book of Genesis is highly selective; what was important to the writer was Abram's relationship with God.

We do not know how Abram first came to believe in God. But Genesis does show how his faith revolutionized his life. Abram believed that God had told him to leave Harran and go into Canaan, his intended destination when he left Ur, promising him both land and many descendants. Abram first showed his faith by obeying God, but it was not an unthinking faith and he did not undertake something extraordinary. As he travelled in Canaan, he discovered that settlements provided security for many of the people. But he made his home in tents and relied on God for his security.

Genesis 12:1-4

Problems of faith

Genesis 15:1-2

Abram had adopted his servant, Eliezer, before the promise that he was to be the ancestor of a great nation was given. The promise, however, was that Abram would have a son of his own; Eliezer was not to be his heir.

For fourteen years after this promise, there is no record in the Bible that God spoke directly to Abram. Time went by.

Abram believed in a God whose character is firm and unshakeable, like these mountains near Jericho.

Far right: Ur of the Chaldees was a rich and well-fortified city in Abram's time. Houses there had two floors, but only narrow slits for windows. This cut-away reconstruction shows the main rooms and open roof-space. In the foreground is a chapel where food was offered to the gods.

Abram and Sarai were getting old, and no son was born. Sarai then suggested that an heir might be born if Abram followed the second custom and took Hagar, her maid, as a substitute wife. He did so, and she had a son whom they called Ishmael. Abram must have felt very helpless during this time. He had tried everything he knew in an attempt to fulfil God's promise and still hoped that Sarai would have a son of her own.

Genesis 16:16, 17:1

What happened next illustrates two important aspects of the religion of the early Israelites. First, Abram had a new vision of God, who called himself 'El Shaddai', God Almighty. The words probably meant 'the God of the mountains', which would have taught Abram to think of God as fully reliable, as a mountain is solid and unchanging. Belief in a God who was sufficient to change hopeless situations was to become a central feature of Israel's faith.

Genesis 17:1

The second thing that happened was that Abram's name was changed to Abraham, and Sarai's to Sarah. In the Bible a new name is frequently a symbol of a changed character; God is sometimes shown intervening in situations by changing people rather than circumstances. From now on, Abraham's faith in God became increasingly wholehearted. As a result, the promise that he would become the father of a great nation began to come true. Sarah had a son, Isaac.

Genesis 17:5,15

Isaac's wife, Rebekah, came from the area of Harran, where Abraham had settled after leaving Ur. After a wait of 20 years they had twin boys, Jacob and Esau, and the promise to Abraham continued through Jacob. He was to have twelve sons and perhaps the one most remembered is Joseph, his favourite.

Genesis 24

Genesis 37:2

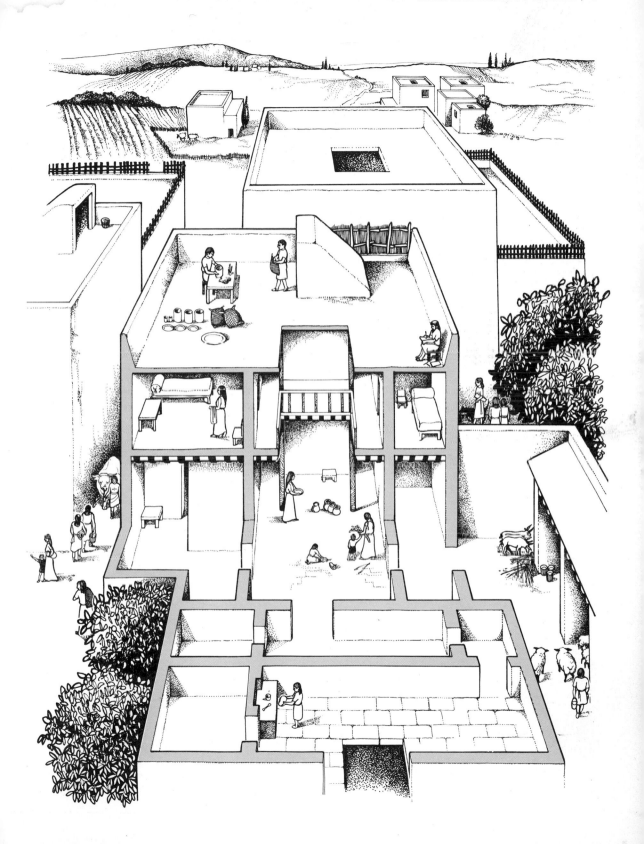

Sumer: cradle of civilization

The Sumerians were an energetic and inventive people who had a great and lasting influence on the cultural development of the Near East.

Below: a Sumerian battle-scene portrayed on the mosaic panels of the 'Standard of Ur'.

They settled in the broad valley region of Mesopotamia (a name meaning 'the land between two rivers') around 4000 BC. Their original habitation is unknown.

When the Tigris and Euphrates rivers flooded each year they deposited mud and silt to form a fertile green strip across land which was otherwise unproductive desert. The Sumerians built canals and dams to regulate the water-supply and

been discovered at Ur, one of the largest and wealthiest of the Sumerian cities, are made from raw materials not found in the area. Gold, copper, ivory, precious woods and fine stone were all imported and made into household implements and ornaments by the skilled Sumerian craftsmen.

As trade and commerce became important, the Sumerians devised a system of

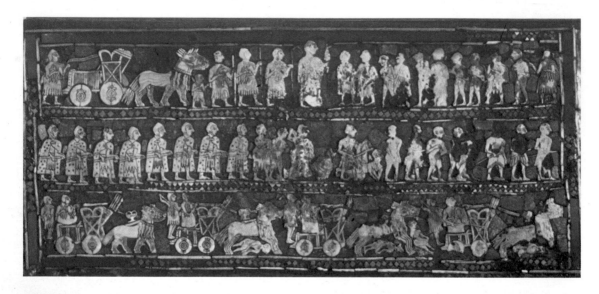

Sumerian craftsmen were highly skilled. The golden containers (right) and delicate jewellery (below) are examples of their work.

successful irrigation agriculture became their chief source of wealth. The farmers produced a food surplus, so that the society could support people who were not directly involved in growing crops or rearing cattle. A new class of craftsmen, builders, priests and scribes emerged and the Sumerian cities became the first centres of civilized society.

While the Sumerians could provide all their own food and clothing, other things had to be imported. Treasures which have

book-keeping. They recorded sales and purchases by drawing pictures of the objects on clay tablets. Over some 500 years, these simple 'pictographs' developed into signs representing whole words or syllables. These signs became the first form of writing in the usual sense, called 'cuneiform', meaning 'wedge-shaped'.

The Sumerians were also expert mathematicians, counting in tens and sixties. Their system has been adopted in the modern division of a circle into 360 degrees, an hour into sixty minutes, and a minute into sixty seconds.

Sumerians went to school in the temples where they learnt cuneiform writing, maths, applied geometry and simple astronomy. Some of the students would later become architects or doctors; the medical knowledge of the day was a mixture of surgery, herbal treatments and magic!

Each city had its own god as its 'patron' and special protector. Ur, for instance, was the centre of worship of the moon-god who they called Nannar. (The god's name of 'Sin' was used by the Semitic people.) The religion was one of fear, and the priests made daily sacrifices to appease the anger of the gods. Sometimes worshippers would leave little statuettes of themselves in the temple to pray on their behalf. Civil and religious life were closely linked in Sumerian society. The king or governor was often a high priest and was sometimes even regarded as a god.

The rulers of Sumer, with their efficient army and advanced weapons, were able to extend and control a powerful empire. Sumer, unlike Egypt, never became a strong unified nation but remained a confederation of separate city-states. Eventually, a long period of war between the Mesopotamian city-states was ended by King Hammurabi, who became ruler of Bábylon in 1792 BC. He began a campaign of imperial conquest and swept south to the Persian Gulf, overwhelming the already weakened Sumerians.

The Sumerian influence lived on, however, even if the nation itself disappeared. The Babylonians adopted many features of the conquered civilization. The last Sumerian attempt at restoring their shattered empire was a revolt in the reign of Hammurabi's son, but it failed.

Joseph the dreamer

Genesis 37

Joseph was his father Jacob's favourite son – and that made him the butt of his brothers' jealousy. He told them about his dreams in which they had all bowed to his authority. This made them so angry that they plotted to kill him. At the last minute they decided to profit from his misfortune, and sold him as a slave to some travelling merchants. He was taken to Egypt, and the brothers told their father that Joseph had been killed by wild animals.

Genesis 39:1-6

Potiphar, one of the Pharaoh's army officers, bought Joseph, and when he proved an above-average slave put him in charge of the household. A slave in Egypt did not always have a harsh life, especially if, like Joseph, he worked in a private house rather than as a labourer on the royal building sites.

Genesis 39:7-23

But his comparative freedom did not last long. Potiphar's wife attempted to seduce Joseph and when he did not respond to her advances, she claimed that he had tried to attack her. Potiphar, believing that Joseph had taken advantage of his trust, threw him into prison.

Genesis 40, 41

In jail, Joseph gained a reputation for telling his fellow prisoners, who included Pharaoh's baker and butler, the

Joseph organized food collection and distribution in famine-stricken Egypt. This Egyptian tomb painting from about 1400 BC shows officials assessing crops.

meaning of their dreams. Two years later, when the butler was back in favour at court, Pharaoh himself had a dream which worried him. The butler mentioned Joseph, who was summoned to interpret Pharaoh's dream. It predicted, said Joseph, a long and severe famine. The only solution was to store and ration grain.

His insight led to his appointment as Minister of Agriculture and Chief Economic Adviser in charge of the rationing. It was not in fact unusual for slaves to reach such high positions of trust or for foreigners to hold government office in Egypt at that time. Joseph himself believed that God had brought him through his many difficulties in order to save both Egypt and his family from starvation.

Genesis 42–45

The famine, when it came, was felt in Canaan too, the country where Joseph's family still lived. His brothers had heard that there was corn in Egypt and went there to buy food. They did not at first recognize Joseph, who engineered some tests to satisfy himself that his brothers had become wiser and

Genesis 46:1-7

kinder men. Then, with Pharaoh's approval, he invited his father and his brothers' families to settle in Egypt. This may have been during the time that invaders from Palestine, the Hyksos, ruled Egypt. The Hyksos may have had some connections with the wandering descendants of Abraham, and contemporary paintings show Semites of the same period as Joseph arriving in Egypt.

The early ancestors of the Jewish people were now in Egypt and the stage was set for the next important act in their history.

The shepherd-kings of Egypt

Groups of people known as the Hyksos emigrated to Egypt from Palestine and settled in the eastern part of the Nile Delta. They were sometimes known as the 'shepherd kings', but their name actually means 'foreign chiefs'. They gradually extended their influence southwards to Memphis and part of the Nile Valley. By about 1720 BC, Hyksos warriors had conquered most of Egypt and they controlled the country for much of the seventeenth century BC.

The Hyksos generally showed respect for the Egyptian civilization. They adopted Egyptian titles and habits, and used hieroglyphs to write their names. Burial customs remained unchanged and the Egyptian god Seth was still worshipped because it was identified with Baal, the Hyksos god.

They did, however, introduce several new ideas and techniques. They used bronze instead of copper for their implements. They also imported into Egypt hump-backed cattle and possibly the small horse, the vertical loom, the lyre and the lute. They greatly influenced ancient Egyptian attitudes to warfare and conquest. Their use of light, horse-drawn two-wheeled chariots revolutionized Egyptian battle-lines, giving the troops great speed and mobility. From the time of the Hyksos, Egypt kept a fully-trained, professional army, and began using its military strength to build up an empire.

A new line of Egyptian-born rulers came to power in Thebes about 1650 BC. They still paid tribute to the Hyksos but preserved their independence. It was these princes of Thebes who, in 1570 BC, eventually overthrew the Hyksos, drove them out of Egypt and established the New Kingdom under Ahmose I.

Escape to freedom

Slaves in Egypt

Jacob's descendants stayed in Egypt for over four centuries, and during that time grew into a large nation. But by the time Moses was born, about 1350 BC, the Hebrews were no longer Pharaoh's guests. They were his slaves.

A fresh and colourful chapter of Egyptian history began when Ahmose became Pharaoh after driving the Hyksos out of Egypt in 1570 BC. For four hundred years the country prospered. Splendid new buildings were erected, and the army was re-organized and well-trained. The building projects for great cities such as Pithom and Raamses needed labourers, and the Hebrews were soon forced to become brick-makers. Some Hebrews may have been slaves during the reign of Ahmose I (1570–1546 BC), but the most unpleasant period was under Sethos I (1317–1290 BC) and Ramesses II (1290–1224 BC).

Exodus 5

They worked under severe conditions. Their Egyptian foremen were harsh, denying them the straw they badly needed for their work. Even Egyptian records of the period tell a similar story. But the Hebrews continued to increase in

The River Nile is essential for irrigation and transport in Egypt. This is the traditional river craft, the felucca.

Exodus 1:15-22

spite of the harsh treatment. In an attempt to reduce their numbers the Egyptians made a law which said that all Hebrew boys were to be killed at birth.

Birth of a leader

Exodus 2:1-10

Moses was born about this time to Amram and Jochabed, who belonged to the tribe of Levi. Shortly after his birth his mother put him in a basket made from papyrus reeds and hid him in the rushes beside the Nile. An Egyptian princess found him, adopted him, and brought him up as an Egyptian at the royal court. In fact, she unknowingly employed the boy's mother as a nurse for a time.

Life in ancient Egypt was leisurely and luxurious for the rich. This fifteenth-century BC tomb painting shows guests at a banquet.

Moses was probably educated either by the priests at Heliopolis or by a private teacher who would have been a court officer. He would have been taught to read and write the hieroglyphic script and trained for a position in the Egyptian Civil Service. Studies in letter-writing and the handling of state matters took their place alongside physical training and archery. Egyptian documents show that what happened to Moses was not unusual. Many foreigners were brought up in or around the royal palaces and trained for official work.

Exodus 2:15

Exodus 2:21

Moses became aware of the sufferings of his own Hebrew people during his time at court, but after killing an Egyptian who was beating a slave, he fled to Midian for safety. Here he met Jethro, a Midianite priest, and married one of his daughters, Zipporah; they had a son, Gershom. Moses settled happily in Midian, and learned much about desert life that later proved valuable. But he did not forget that the Hebrews were suffering harsh treatment in Egypt.

Exodus 3:11,14;
4:1,10,13

His court and desert experiences made Moses an ideal person to lead the Hebrews in a bid for freedom. But when he first became aware of the possibility of leadership, he put forward five reasons why he was unsuitable for it. He felt he was too insignificant a person; he did not have a sufficiently close relationship with God; he had no confidence that the

Hebrews would believe that God had sent him to be their leader; he was not a good public speaker; and he simply felt inadequate for the task.

But as he prayed, each objection was met with a fresh reassurance: God would help him. As Abraham had a new vision of God at a time of crisis, so too did Moses. He learned a new name for God: Yahweh. It meant that God was the Lord, or king, of the nation. The God of Abraham, Isaac and Jacob was to be the God of Moses and the Hebrews.

Exodus 3:13-15

At last Moses went to Egypt with his brother Aaron to meet the Hebrew leaders. Then they went to face Pharaoh. Ramesses II, who may have been Pharaoh at the time, allowed such interviews. Moses' mission to secure the release of the Hebrews from Egypt failed, however, and their work conditions were made worse.

Ramesses II added these colossal statues of himself to the Luxor temple, built by an earlier ruler.

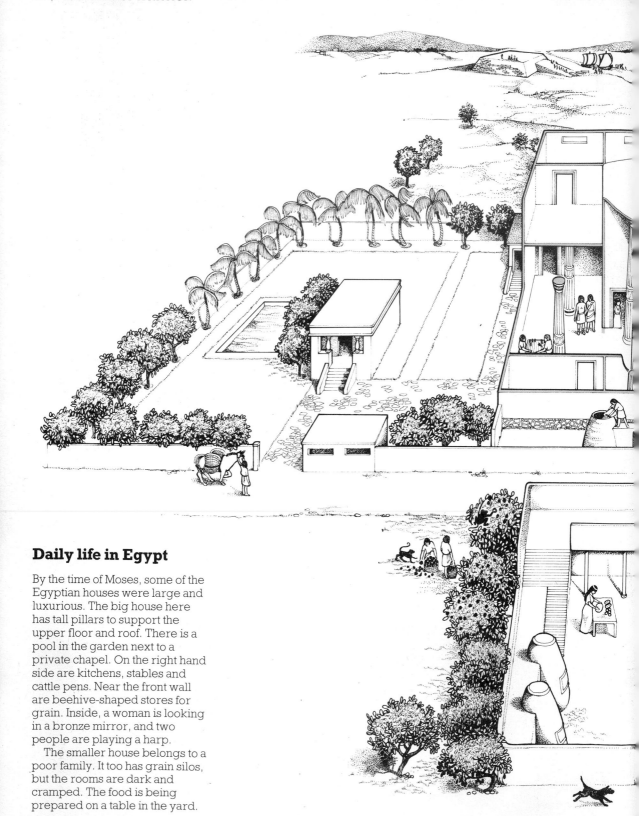

Daily life in Egypt

By the time of Moses, some of the
Egyptian houses were large and
luxurious. The big house here
has tall pillars to support the
upper floor and roof. There is a
pool in the garden next to a
private chapel. On the right hand
side are kitchens, stables and
cattle pens. Near the front wall
are beehive-shaped stores for
grain. Inside, a woman is looking
in a bronze mirror, and two
people are playing a harp.

The smaller house belongs to a
poor family. It too has grain silos,
but the rooms are dark and
cramped. The food is being
prepared on a table in the yard.

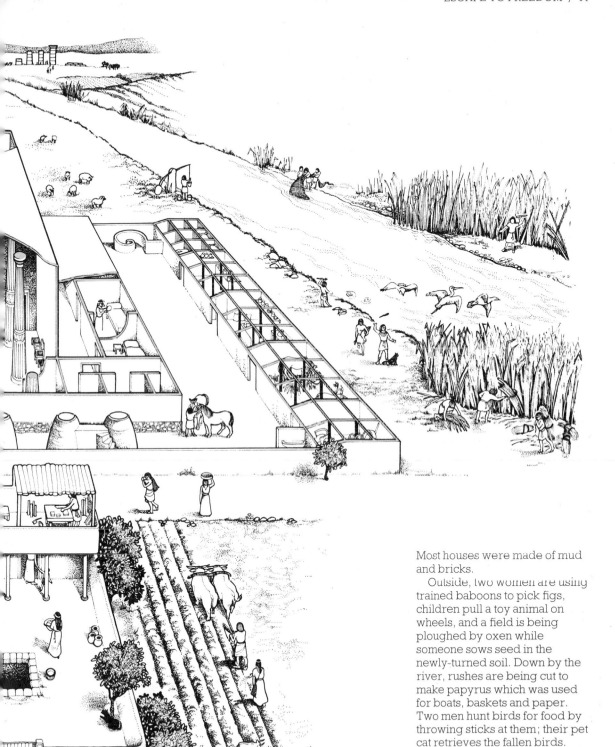

Most houses were made of mud and bricks.

Outside, two women are using trained baboons to pick figs, children pull a toy animal on wheels, and a field is being ploughed by oxen while someone sows seed in the newly-turned soil. Down by the river, rushes are being cut to make papyrus which was used for boats, baskets and paper. Two men hunt birds for food by throwing sticks at them; their pet cat retrieves the fallen birds. Nearby a nobleman is spearing fish, while on the far bank fishermen use a net. In the background, a team of slaves is building a pyramid.

The exodus

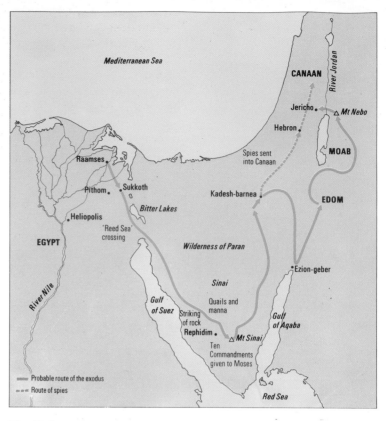

Map labels:
Mediterranean Sea
CANAAN
River Jordan
Jericho
△ Mt Nebo
Hebron
MOAB
Raamses
Spies sent into Canaan
Pithom
Sukkoth
Bitter Lakes
Kadesh-barnea
EDOM
Heliopolis
'Reed Sea' crossing
EGYPT
Wilderness of Paran
Ezion-geber
River Nile
Sinai
Gulf of Suez
Quails and manna
Striking of rock
Gulf of Aqaba
Rephidim
△ Mt Sinai
Ten Commandments given to Moses
Red Sea
Probable route of the exodus
Route of spies

The exodus

The Hebrews did finally escape from Egypt, but only after a series of ten plagues. The plagues were a direct challenge to the gods of Egypt, and showed how helpless they were compared with the God of the Hebrews.

The slaves hurriedly prepared for their escape. They begged gold, silver and clothing from their captors, then, when the first-born sons of Egyptian families died in the final plague, they set out. The night before they left they ate the first 'Passover' meal, to celebrate the fact that God had 'passed over' or spared their sons and was about to liberate them. The Passover feast is celebrated by Jews every year as a reminder of this great event in their history.

Exodus 12

The Hebrews probably left Egypt about 1280 BC. They threw off their pursuers by crossing the Yam Suph or 'Reedy Sea' (not the Red Sea) in the marshes between the Bitter Lakes and the town of Zilu, and went into the desert (or wilderness) on their way to Canaan, the 'promised land'. They were disorganized and owned little equipment, yet they believed that God had delivered them and would lead them. It was easy to say this at the beginning of a journey with the dramatic events of the 'exodus' or departure still fresh in their minds. It was quite another matter to go on believing it when life became hard in the desert.

The Hebrews could not travel along the coastal road to

Canaan because Egyptian forts guarded it. So they had to turn into the desert where there was little food, water or shelter from the hot sun. The greenery of Egypt became a memory that hurt in the dry and difficult desert. The gulf of salty water on the west was useless for drinking, but it made their thirst harder to bear. Moses was blamed for these problems and the complaints came thick and fast. But he still believed God would help the people – and a number of solutions to the problems were given.

Exodus 16:4-12

First, they discovered manna on the ground, which they ate. It was a sugary substance, about the size of a pea, probably secreted by a desert insect. It became sticky and edible in the heat of the sun. Secondly, migrating quails landed in the

Exodus 16:13

desert. They had flown long distances, had become tired in flight and were easily caught, cooked and eaten.

The lack of water was the biggest and most pressing

Exodus 17:1-6

problem. But at Rephidim, Moses prayed, and then struck one of the many porous rocks which often contain water in the Sinai desert. Water flowed out of it, and there was enough for the whole company. As a result the people's faith in the God who had saved them became stronger.

Exodus 19:20

Near the desert home of Jethro, Moses climbed Mt Sinai to meet God and to receive from him instructions for the future life of the Hebrews. They included the Ten Commandments, detailed instructions about the social life of the nation, and plans for the tent of meeting, which was to become the centre of their worship. The tribes remained at the foot of the mountain in the cool shade with plenty of water to drink from the oasis.

Journey's end

The Hebrews had come to Sinai as a rabble of refugees. They left it with a new purpose in life and a clear faith. They were to be the people of the God who had rescued them from Egypt. And he had a land for them to occupy.

From the mountains of Moab, Moses looked across into the land of Canaan. This view, from the western side of the Dead Sea, is of the hills of Moab in modern-day Jordan.

Numbers 13,14

Sinai had not been the goal, but only a step along the way. When the tribes arrived at Kadesh-barnea, Moses sent twelve spies into Canaan. In spite of encouragement from two of them, Joshua and Caleb, the majority voted against invading the land. They said that the task was too difficult, the Canaanites were too strong, their cities too well fortified. Sadly, Moses led the people back into the desert and there they stayed for another thirty-eight years.

Moses stood on the mountains of Moab and looked into the 'promised land'. He had learned that El Shaddai, the God of Abraham, who is all-sufficient, is also Yahweh, the God of the nation, active and present to save and help his people, controlling nature and history and bringing joy and power. But Moses' work was over. His brother Aaron and his sister Miriam had both died, and his own life was almost at an end.

About 1240 BC a new crisis faced the Hebrews. They could not stay in the desert for ever; they had to conquer Canaan. Moses handed over the leadership of the people to Joshua, who dedicated himself to the task of securing a new homeland for them.

The covenant

Covenants, or agreements between people, were a common feature of social life two millennia before Christ. They were a form of contract binding both parties, made with an oath and sometimes sealed by an exchange of tokens of good faith.

The Bible records several covenants between God and the Hebrews. The first was with Noah after the flood, in which God promised that the world would never again be totally destroyed by water. Then there was the covenant with Abraham, that he should be the father of a great nation. Jesus Christ spoke of 'the new covenant in my blood' just before his crucifixion. The New Testament interprets his words in terms of the restored relationship between men and God which his death was to achieve. But none of these

Unlike a human agreement in which both sides bargain over the terms, God set out his unchangeable laws in his covenant with Moses.

covenants was like a human contract, because there could be no equality between the two parties. Although freely entered into by the people concerned, the covenants originated from a God who himself laid down the terms.

The covenant between Moses and God can be summed up in two parts: 'I will be your God' and 'You shall be my people'. The future of the Hebrews was to be built on this. God had given them freedom and from now on they were to serve him by obeying his laws and teaching them to the world. According to Deuteronomy 7:7-8, they were chosen not because of merit but because of their need. Now their task was to serve others.

The covenant embodied new concepts in the Hebrew understanding of God. He was seen as being active in history, a God who did things which could be dated in time and located on a map. All biblical history is like this. But God had not been chosen by the Hebrews themselves. Rather, he had chosen them. They depended on God, but he did not depend on them. Other nations at the time regarded their gods as mainly concerned with making crops grow and giving good harvests. If one of these nations was defeated in a battle, then so was the god. With the Hebrews it was different; God was never defeated, even if they were.

The covenant at Sinai was not an agreement between two equal parties. God loved a people who had been helpless slaves. Because he loved them, God longed that the Hebrews should love him in return and so enjoy his protection and help. This faith was to lie at the very heart of their religion, and it still does lie at the heart of Christianity. The laws and ceremonies of religion were the result of a loving trust in a God who had acted to save his people. The Ten Commandments begin: 'I am the Lord your God who brought you out of the land of Egypt, out of the house of bondage.' God gave them their freedom; only afterwards did he ask for their obedience.

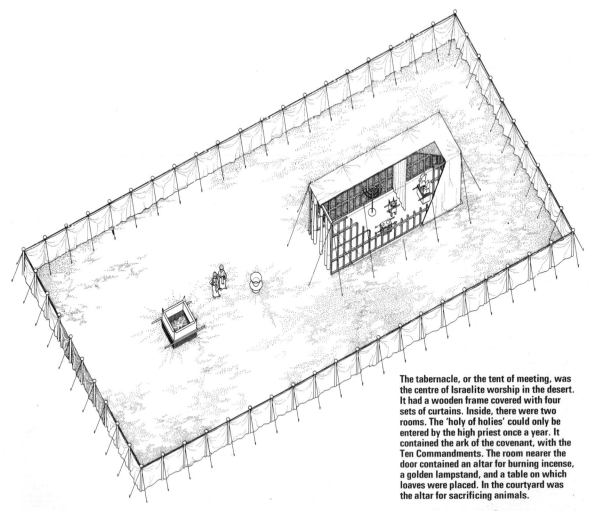

The tabernacle, or the tent of meeting, was the centre of Israelite worship in the desert. It had a wooden frame covered with four sets of curtains. Inside, there were two rooms. The 'holy of holies' could only be entered by the high priest once a year. It contained the ark of the covenant, with the Ten Commandments. The room nearer the door contained an altar for burning incense, a golden lampstand, and a table on which loaves were placed. In the courtyard was the altar for sacrificing animals.

Settling in Canaan

Moses was dead. The new leader, Joshua, had the huge task of conquering and possessing Canaan. The Hebrews had been used to a wandering life. They had not built cities to live in and they knew little about farming. Under Joshua they had not only to conquer the land, but to learn to live a settled life. And at the same time, they would have to mix with peoples whose ways of life were very different from their own.

A new leader

As Joshua faced these problems, he must have been glad of the training that he had received under Moses. Moses had discovered that being a leader is not an easy job. He knew what it was like to be lonely, to be picked on and blamed by the very people he wanted to help. But his faith in God had given him the strength and courage to carry on. And as Joshua

Joshua 1:5

began his work he became aware of God's promise: 'As I was with Moses so will I be with you. I will not fail you nor forsake you.'

Joshua 3:14-17

The first problem was to cross the River Jordan and establish a foothold in Canaan. The river was broad and there were no bridges, but a crossing became possible when the Jordan briefly dried up. It may have been blocked by a landslide upstream (something which has been known to happen more recently – in 1906 and again in 1927); but the Hebrews saw it as God's work. They set up a monument of stones taken from the river bed to remind them of what had happened.

The city of Jericho was near where the crossing had been

Below: this defensive tower at Jericho is possibly the oldest building in the world.

Below right: different levels of settlement excavated at old Jericho, dating to about 8000 BC. The modern town is in the background.

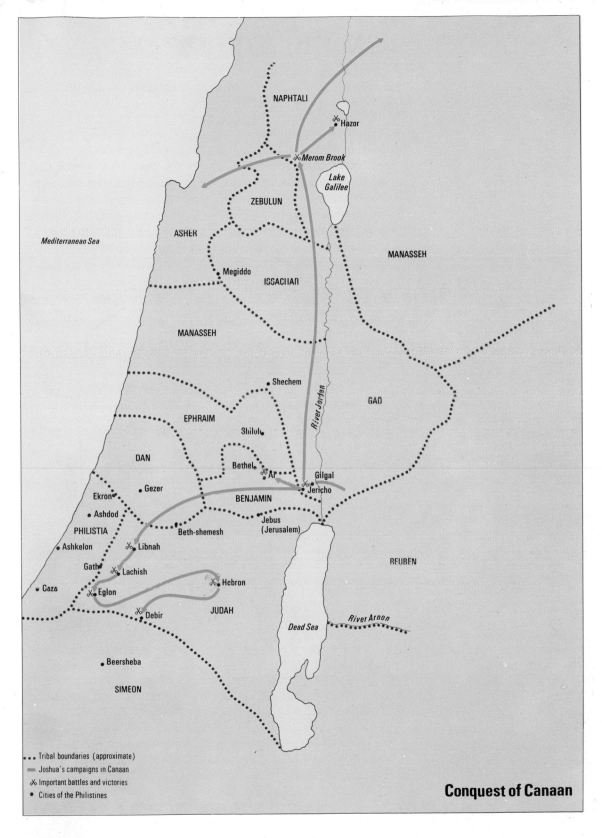

NAPHTALI

⚔ Hazor

⚔ Merom Brook

Lake Galilee

ZEBULUN

ASHER

Mediterranean Sea

MANASSEH

• Megiddo

ISSACHAR

MANASSEH

• Shechem

River Jordan

GAD

EPHRAIM

• Shiloh

DAN

Bethel •

⚔ Ai

Gilgal

• Gezer

Jericho

Ekron •

BENJAMIN

• Ashdod

Jebus (Jerusalem)

PHILISTIA

Beth-shemesh

• Ashkelon

⚔ Libnah

Gath •

REUBEN

⚔ Lachish

Gaza •

⚔ Eglon

⚔ Hebron

⚔ Debir

JUDAH

Dead Sea

River Arnon

• Beersheba

SIMEON

••• Tribal boundaries (approximate)
— Joshua's campaigns in Canaan
⚔ Important battles and victories
• Cities of the Philistines

Conquest of Canaan

Genesis 32:27-28

made. News had already reached the inhabitants that the Israelites, as they were now called, were coming, and they were afraid. 'Israel' was the new name that was given to Jacob. After the exodus this term was generally used to describe the tribes which were now linked together as one nation under the covenant.

There had been a city at the site of Jericho since about 8000 BC. By Joshua's time it was walled and well-defended, yet the people did not feel secure against these invaders. They had heard that a powerful God was with Israel. But Joshua did not imagine that Jericho would simply open its gates and allow

Joshua 2:1-24

the Israelites in. Before he had crossed the Jordan he had sent two spies to explore the city and surrounding country. The two men were almost captured, but they escaped with the help of a woman from Jericho called Rahab. They reported that although the city was strongly fortified, it could be captured.

Conquest

Jericho fell, and from then on the Israelites swept through Canaan in a series of fast-moving campaigns. They moved through the centre and east of the country first, later spreading south and north. They put out of action a number of Canaanite city-states, giving themselves time to develop and consolidate their captured territories.

But it was one thing to defeat a number of minor kings and their small armies; it was quite another to settle into the conquered land, learn to occupy it, breed cattle on it and farm it, as well as building new cities to live in. The early victories needed following up and the land had to be made safe. Joshua

Joshua 13:1-6

and his people began this, but left 'much land to be taken'.

Archaeologists have discovered that many cities, including Hazor, Debir and Lachish, were destroyed between 1240 and 1200 BC. The Israelites are the people most likely to have caused the destruction. But the conquest was still far from complete, and cities such as Jerusalem, Megiddo, Gezer and Beth-shemesh remained untaken for some years. Jerusalem (at this time called Jebus) did not fall, in fact, until the reign of King David, some 200 years later.

Settling into Canaan proved to be a difficult venture. Would the God who had guided them in the desert be able to help them in their new surroundings? Or should they turn to Baal, the god of the Canaanites who knew about farming and city life, and mix his worship with that of Yahweh? Joshua, aware that the Israelites could forget the promises made to God in the desert, called the tribes together at Shechem. By this time he

Joshua 24:2-15

was an old man who had fought hard battles. He reminded the people of their past history and called them to renew the covenant with God. There was to be no mixing of the religion of Israel with that of the Canaanites.

Joshua had finished an important and difficult task. The Israelites were in their new homeland, but the tribes were

The Israelites, accustomed to the hardships of nomadic life, now faced the new challenge of settled agricultural life in Canaan.

scattered loosely over the country and needed strong organization. The tent of meeting and the box (or ark) containing the laws, which were symbols of the unity of Israel and central to its religion, were placed at Shechem then later moved to Shiloh. But would the people retain their foothold? Failure to do so meant destruction. The tribes were cut off from close contact with one another, because of the rough and difficult countryside. They were living among nations with different beliefs and cultures. Would they be able to take over Canaan, or would Canaan take them over?

Joshua died before this question could be answered, and for almost 200 years the Israelites failed to find a powerful leader with the ability of either Moses or Joshua.

Sea-borne invaders

A Philistine soldier, wearing a plumed head-dress with a chin-strap.

The Philistines posed a serious threat to Israel's security for many generations. As one of the many groups of 'sea peoples', probably from the Aegean area, the Philistines were dominant in a wave of immigrants to the Near East in the twelfth century BC. They attacked many parts of the Mediterranean coasts. They even tried to invade Egypt but were defeated in a sea battle.

After their defeat, some Philistine soldiers acted as mercenary troops for the pharaohs; others turned their attention to Canaan and about 1175 BC they settled along part of the coastal plain. There may have been small groups of Philistines already living on the southern edges of Canaan when the Israelites left Egypt in about 1280 BC, causing them to detour inland. The invasion was on a far bigger scale than any previous settlement attempts.

The Israelites did not encounter the Philistines during the actual conquest of Canaan. But by the time Joshua was an old man, Philistia comprised the five cities in the south-west of the country: Ashdod, Ashkelon, Ekron, Gath and Gaza, and also the coastal strip south of Carmel, extending eastwards to the foothills of Judah.

The Philistines constantly pressed inland, trying to increase their territorial control. Samson, one of the last judges, was one Israelite leader who boldly confronted them. Although his raids were daring, he never managed to free his people from Philistine power.

It was probably largely due to this continuing pressure that Israel demanded a king. They wanted a strong, military leader who would defeat the Philistines once and for all. During the erratic reign of Israel's first king, Saul, they continued to be a major threat; King David, however, drove them out of the hill-country, carried out attacks in Philistia itself and prevented the Philistines being any further serious menace.

Not much is known about the Philistines' way of life. They seem to have adopted the Canaanite religion and culture and the Semitic languages of the peoples whose land they took over. The Old Testament gives Philistine gods Semitic names: Dagon, with temples at Gaza and Ashdod; Baalzebub, worshipped at Ekron; and Ashtoreth (Astarte). The five cities have not all been identified with certainty because many sites in the area are still occupied. No excavated temples can be definitely said to be of Philistine origin. It is known, however, that they offered animal sacrifices and wore charms into battle.

Egyptian carved reliefs show Philistine soldiers wearing head-dresses of feathers rising vertically from a horizontal band. They are armed with lances, round shields, long broadswords and triangular-shaped daggers. Their great advantage was their knowledge of iron-working; the bronze weapons of the Israelites were no match against them.

Philistine pottery dating from 1200 to 1100 BC has been found in Israel, especially at sites on the coast. The pottery is like the Mycenean type made in Greece, Crete and Cyprus and provides some evidence of the link between the Philistines and the Aegean Sea area. Nothing else has been found that can be called 'Philistine' as distinct from Canaanite or Israelite. But although few actual remains of the culture of the Philistines have been discovered, they gave their name – as Palestine – to the whole of the land west of the River Jordan.

Pottery, dating from about 1300 BC, which was found on the site of ancient Hazor.

A Canaanite city

Hazor was one of the largest and strongest fortified cities that Joshua's army had to face. It was an important trading and administrative centre, with a population perhaps as high as 40,000, and at one time covering more than 175 acres.

It was mentioned in Egyptian records in the nineteenth century BC, and in eighteenth-century letters from Mari, in which its importance for the tin trade was noted. The Amarna letters from the fourteenth century refer to its ruler as a king, although he was also under the authority of the Egyptian pharaoh.

Joshua is said to have killed the king, Jabin, and burnt the city. Hazor was indeed destroyed or burnt by invading armies on several occasions. Excavations have shown that one such defeat took place in the thirteenth

Hazor was an impressive and well-fortified city in Joshua's time. These ruins include the later, ninth-century BC storehouses.

century BC, which was about the time that the Israelites came into the area under the leadership of Joshua.

The site of Hazor, known as Tell-el-Qedah, was discovered in 1928 but only fully excavated by teams under Dr Yigael Yadin between 1955 and 1958 and 1968–70. Many different levels of development have been unearthed. Canaanite homes and pottery from the thirteenth

century were found in the south west corner of the site. The city then had several temples and appears to have been at its most prosperous stage.

Later development took place during the reign of Solomon, when he fortified Jerusalem, Hazor and Megiddo. It was finally destroyed during the eighth century BC Assyrian invasion, when the northern kingdom of Israel came to an end.

Food laws and animal sacrifices

The ten commandments provided a summary of the laws which God wanted the Israelites to obey and live by. However, they were also given detailed regulations concerning religious ceremonies, personal hygiene and ownership of property. These are included in the Old Testament book of Leviticus which takes its name from the Levitical priests (members of the tribe of Levi) who were responsible for administering the ritual and laws. A major theme of the book is the holiness of God and the ways in which the people were to maintain their relationship with the 'holy God of Israel'.

Offering sacrifices was a common religious activity in the ancient Near East. While Israel's sacrifices had some similarities with those of neighbouring nations, they had certain unique features. There were no fertility rites, orgies or human sacrifices associated with the Israelite system. No black magic was allowed and the sacrifices were made to Israel's God, Yahweh, and not to several different gods.

The sacrificial system was intended to teach the Israelites certain important truths. Because their God was holy and pure, any kind of 'sin' or wrongdoing broke their special relationship with him. Those who failed to keep his laws or treated other people unfairly had to make an offering to atone – make amends – for the sin committed.

Strict instructions were given about the kind of offering that was acceptable for particular offences: whether it was an animal, bird, grain or oil. It had to be the best that the worshipper could give, because a sacrifice with any defect was not good enough to be offered to God.

Leviticus also contains dietary laws. Orthodox Jews today still adhere to some of these practices and only eat 'kosher' (Hebrew for 'proper' or 'fit') food which has been prepared in a ritually correct way. All meat and poultry must be soaked or salted to remove the blood. Certain foods, such as pork and shellfish, are forbidden.

The original Levitical laws classed food as 'clean' or 'unclean'. Some of the prohibited items are of particular interest in the light of modern knowledge about diet, health and hygiene. Among the banned foods are carnivorous animals, which transmit infection in a warm climate where flesh decays rapidly; pork, which is particularly dangerous in warm climates as pigs are hosts to various parasites; vermin and predatory birds, which are often disease-carriers; and shellfish which even today sometimes cause food-poisoning.

The Israelites were given instructions about the prevention of food and water contamination. These principles still govern public health regulations today. There were also rules of strict cleanliness in all sexual matters, as a positive safeguard for health. The priests acted as doctors for the Israelites and were responsible for diagnosing disease. The laws concerning

isolating people suffering from infectious illnesses are among the earliest quarantine regulations discovered in the Near East.

The people of Israel were also commanded to show concern for the poor and underprivileged, and to be known for their honesty, justice and fair dealing. This was a way of reflecting the character of their God to the surrounding nations. Someone whose circumstances forced him to sell his land retained the right to buy it back within a certain period. Loans without interest were to be made to fellow Israelites who became poor and could not support themselves. The jubilee (fiftieth) year was a time when those who had sold property – and even themselves as slaves – had their freedom and property restored. Even the land itself was not forgotten; the fields were to be left fallow every

seventh year so that the soil would not become exhausted through over-cropping.

Many of the laws which seem strange at first in fact harmonize with the natural working of principles which we now partly understand. And the rituals and rules were never an end in themselves. They reminded the Israelites that their God was holy and that he demanded holiness in his people too.

Only a few small Christian groups have considered the detailed Old Testament food regulations to be binding on them. But all Christians have seen in the death and resurrection of Jesus Christ an act which removes the necessity for any acts of sacrifice to atone for wrongdoing. Jewish sacrifices in fact ended some forty years after Jesus' death when the Romans destroyed the Jerusalem temple.

The Israelites' law did not allow them to eat pork.

Problems of unity

The Israelites had conquered a good deal of the hill country of Canaan by the time Joshua died. They had also occupied most of the Jordan Valley and a large part of the Transjordan plateau. Down on the coastal plains, however, things were different. The people there went into battle with iron chariots and were skilled horsemen.

Because the Israelites fought only on foot they did not dare invade the coastal areas or the Plain of Esdraelon. Those who did venture into these regions either were defeated or they simply joined up with the Canaanites who lived there. Tribes such as Issachar, Zebulun and Naphtali were thus cut off from the rest of Israel by the Canaanites. Even in the mountains there were powerful groups Israel had not been able to overcome.

Judges 1:31-32

The landscape of Canaan made it hard for the tribes to keep together. Not only were those in the Plain of Esdraelon cut off from the rest by the Canaanites, but the deep Jordan Valley separated the eastern tribes from those who lived in the west. The hill country too, was divided by deep valleys making contact between the tribes even more difficult. As a result the tribes became much more concerned about their own local affairs and customs than the needs of the whole nation. The one bond that held them together was their belief in the God of Israel, and their worship of him at the Shiloh tabernacle.

The tribes, then, were aware that they belonged to one nation, but there was no practical expression of that unity except the central place of worship. There was no capital city and no king. Most other nations had their kings at this time, but for the Israelites the important men of each tribe acted as leaders. No national hero like Moses or Joshua emerged and so, when the tribes were attacked and Israel's life was in danger, a local leader or 'judge' would come forward to help the people.

The book of Judges records the exploits of twelve men and one woman who acted as leaders. They differed from one another greatly, but they all had one thing in common. Both they and the people believed that the judges were chosen by God and filled with his Spirit in order to undertake the super-human task of saving Israel from its enemies. As there was no standing army, each judge had to recruit soldiers from the able-bodied men when they needed to defend their homes or attack their enemies. Every fit man was expected to fight if called on, but many people did not respond wholeheartedly.

Judges 5

The poem of Deborah, the only woman judge, describes a battle which was won despite the fact that several tribes refused their support.

Battles with the surrounding nations, including the fierce Philistines, were only a part of Israel's problems. The time of the judges saw the start of another battle, which was to continue for many years, between the God of Israel (Yahweh) and the Canaanite god Baal. The Israelites were not in danger of forgetting their God; rather they had started to confuse him with Baal. They were putting Yahweh, the creator, on a level with Canaanite idols created by men. The judges constantly warned the people about this; they were religious as well as military leaders.

Judges 6:25-32

The story of Gideon shows how the struggle was beginning to develop. His father built an altar to Baal, and when Gideon pulled it down one night there was almost a riot the next day. The worship of Yahweh as the only God was being seriously threatened by the attitude of many people.

But despite these problems, the standard of living in Israel rose steadily. By the eleventh century BC they had learned the building and farming skills which they had not previously needed while they had been wandering in the desert. Forests were being cleared from several regions to provide more land for farming.

The continued military pressure and religious decline meant that Israel needed to establish a new and better organization for the tribes dispersed across the country if it was to survive. Greater co-operation was needed. But they also needed to maintain their faith in Yahweh. The attacks of other nations had already taught that disobedience to the covenant and the adoption of pagan gods brought disaster. But each time the danger was averted, the tribes turned back to their own interests and forgot God. Israel needed a strong leader who would obey God, building the new society on faith in him rather than simply on human ideals.

The mountains of Gilead, across the Jordan Valley, were originally the territory of the tribe of Gad. There was often a lack of unity and cohesion among the tribes partly because of their geographical separation.

Who were the judges?

A clear pattern of events can be seen in the book of Judges. After a period of peace, the Israelites drifted into worshipping the Canaanite gods. For this they were punished as their enemies attacked and defeated them. They cried to God for help and a leader – a judge – emerged who led them to military victory and moral and religious reformation. This cycle is repeated many times, and the book records the names of twelve judges.

Othniel
Judges 3:9-11
The younger brother of Caleb, he defeated an invasion from Hittite-controlled Mesopotamia. The victory heralded forty years of peace.

Ehud
Judges 3:15-30
The Moabites were the next to oppress Israel, having joined with the Ammonites and Amalekites. Ehud killed the Moabite king then led Israel into battle against 10,000 soldiers. They won, and eighty years' peace followed.

Shamgar
Judges 3:31
He is not described as a judge, and may have been a Canaanite. He had limited success against the Philistines, killing 600 of them single-handed.

Deborah
Judges 4:4–5:31
The only woman judge, she was largely a civil leader but also the inspiration behind Barak, the military commander. The army of Hazor was defeated, and forty years of peace followed.

Gideon
Judges 6:11–8:32
The Midianites (from the East) had swept through southern Israel as far as the Philistine city of Gaza. About 1170 BC Gideon scored a decisive victory with a tiny band of 300 soldiers. He refused the invitation to become a king over Israel, and forty years of peace followed.

Tola, Jair
Judges 10:1-5
These were two minor judges during periods of relative peace. Tola picked up the pieces left after three years' chaotic rule by Abimelech who made himself king of Israel.

Jephthah
Judges 11:1–12:7
The Ammonites attacked the eastern borders of Israel, and the Philistines attacked the west. Jephthah freed the eastern tribes but was unable to deal with the Philistines.

Ibzar, Elon, Abdon
Judges 12:8-15
Each enjoyed comparative peace, but the Philistine threat continued to grow.

Samson
Judges 13:21–16:31
He judged Israel for twenty years, and is best known for his feats of strength. In fact, although he scored several spectacular personal victories over the Philistines he was never able to organize an army to fight them. Rather, he did things such as setting fire to fields and slaying soldiers with the jawbone of an ass. He ruled wisely and fairly over local disputes.

The story of Ruth

The judges ruled in violent and uncertain times but life in Israel was not all fighting and bloodshed. Most of the people just carried on working to provide food, clothing and shelter for themselves and their families. The story of Ruth is a glimpse of social customs at the time.

Sometime during this period, a famine occurred. A man called Elimelech, who lived in Bethlehem, took his wife Naomi and two sons Mahlon and Chilion to Moab, 50 miles (80 km) away on the eastern side of the Dead Sea, where there was more food. The two young Israelites married the Moabite girls Ruth and Orpah. Tragedy hit the family as first Elimelech and then his sons died, leaving three widows with no means of livelihood or hope for the future.

Naomi decided to return to Bethlehem, where relatives would have looked after Elimelech's house and field during the family's ten-year absence. As head of the family, she had a legal right to the service of her two daughters-in-law, but she was also under an obligation to find them husbands. She could not offer prospective husbands good dowries with the young widows, so she gave them their freedom instead. Orpah chose to stay with her family in Moab. But Ruth was determined to go with Naomi back to Israel. She may have given up worshipping the Moabite fertility god Chemosh and wanted to serve the God of Israel she had heard about from her husband.

Naomi and Ruth arrived in Bethlehem in April, at the time of the barley-harvest. It was hard for widows to earn a living but Ruth took advantage of an ancient Jewish law which allowed poor people to collect up corn left for them by the reapers at the side of the field. The land was divided into strips marked by boundary stones. The part of the field in which Ruth worked belonged to Boaz, a wealthy relative of Elimelech.

Once the barley and wheat harvests were over, there would be no means for Ruth and her mother-in-law to earn a living. Naomi felt obliged to help Ruth remarry so that she could raise an heir to carry on the family name. She knew that Boaz would be sleeping out of doors, perhaps to guard his harvest, so she sent Ruth to lie at his feet before he woke up. (There may well have been some accepted custom behind Naomi's strange but detailed instructions.) When Boaz woke, Ruth asked him to spread his cloak over her, symbolically asking him to marry her and provide a son

who could be the legal descendant of her dead father-in-law, Elimelech.

The laws of kinship in Israel gave members of a family a strong obligation to help and protect one another. Boaz accepted Ruth's request, but first of all had to sort out the ownership of the family property with another, closer, relative.

Naomi owned a small piece of land which she wanted to sell and this 'next-of-kin' had to be given the opportunity to buy it. It was the right and duty of a kinsman to buy family property sold by needy relatives. In this case, the deal included marrying Ruth and raising an heir for the dead Elimelech. The next-of-kin was not prepared to take on this responsibility and Boaz was given the right to purchase the field and take Ruth as his wife.

These legal matters and similar business were all transacted in the open square at the city gates with the elders of Bethlehem as official witnesses.

Ruth and Boaz married; their son Obed was King David's grandfather and an ancestor of Jesus, who was also born in Bethlehem hundreds of years later.

The book of Ruth has very little to say about the religion of Israel at this time, but its picture of social customs illustrates the close family ties which have always been a feature of Jewish life. And Ruth has often been taken as an example of someone with a simple but sincere faith in a God who directs people's lives. The book may have reminded the Jews of their obligation to welcome and provide for foreigners.

By gathering the left-over grain at harvest-time, Ruth was able to provide for herself and her mother-in-law, Naomi.

THE GROWTH OF THE KINGDOM

A stable and respected leadership is essential if a large group of people are to live harmoniously. Over the centuries different systems have evolved: monarchies, federations, dictatorships, and so on. For the emergent nation of Israel the style of leadership posed continual problems.

At first, the ideal was for Israel to be a theocracy: God alone was their king. The judges steered the people through a suc-

cession of crises. But the people demanded a more permanent human leadership. They were given the kings they asked for, and a second wave of leaders, the prophets, followed in their wake. Their role as political advisers was related to the task of guarding the nation's religious life. The conflict between the sacred and the secular, between religious devotion and political necessity, had already begun.

The kingdom established

1 Samuel 4

Israel was in chaos. The Philistines posed a constant threat, and eventually routed the Israelite army at Ebenezer. In a last-ditch effort to defend themselves, the Israelites brought the ark of the covenant, the symbol of God's presence, from its sanctuary at Shiloh into their camp on the battlefield. Surely God would rescue them from their enemies now, they thought. But the outcome of the next battle was even worse than the previous one. The ark was captured, Hophni and Phineas, the priests, were killed, and their father Eli died of the resulting shock.

1 Samuel 5

The Philistines did not keep the ark long. They were a superstitious people. When illness, probably spread by a plague of mice, broke out, and the statue of their god Dagon fell flat on its face in front of the ark, they believed that God was

1 Samuel 6

punishing them for taking the ark. So they sent it back to Israel

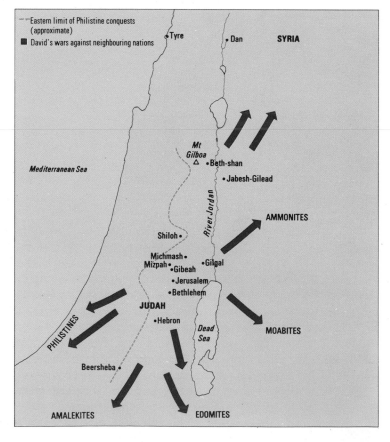

Israel at the time of Saul and David

The Israelites were often tempted to adopt the idols and practices of their Canaanite neighbours, but Samuel encouraged whole-hearted loyalty to the one true God. This Canaanite shrine at Megiddo was in use at a much earlier period, 2500–1500 BC.

and it stayed for many years in the town of Kireath-jearim. Israel's hopes were in ruins and everyone felt that God had forsaken them completely. But not for the last time in the biblical story, a child who grew up to become an outstanding leader was born in unusual circumstances.

Samuel the prophet

Every year a man named Elkanah from the tribe of Ephraim took his two wives, Hannah and Peninnah, to worship at the tabernacle in Shiloh. These visits were unhappy times for Hannah. Unlike Peninnah she had no children and Peninnah teased her cruelly. One year, probably about 1080 BC, when Hannah was praying at the tabernacle, she promised God that if he would give her a son, she would dedicate the boy wholly to God's service. Her prayer was answered and the next year she gave birth to Samuel. When he was about three years old, his mother sent him to Shiloh to serve Eli and to train to become a priest.

1 Samuel 1:9-28

Samuel grew to be very different from Hophni and Phineas. They had given the priesthood a bad name, but Samuel was conscientious and honest. Even old Eli was not entirely without fault. He had never spoken to his sons about their attitude and behaviour, and so he was also partly to blame for their conduct.

1 Samuel 3:2-18

One night, Samuel heard a voice calling his name. He was perhaps about fourteen years old, and thought at first that Eli had called him and wanted him to do something. But Eli had said nothing, and, believing that God might be speaking to the boy, told him to listen again. The voice told Samuel that Eli and his sons were going to be punished by God for their disobedience. It was a difficult message for him to pass on to the high priest. But when Eli heard it, he accepted it as a word from God, and became convinced that Samuel was God's messenger. Shortly afterwards, Eli and his sons were dead.

As the years went on, Samuel's authority grew and people consulted him about all kinds of social, religious and legal problems, as they had the judges before him. He became a leader who offered prayers and sacrifices for the people at Ramah, his home, and regularly visited Shiloh, Bethel and Gilgal to hold courts.

1 Samuel 7:5-14

Samuel was a judge, a priest and a prophet. He knew that Israel could only defeat the Philistines and regain full control of Canaan if the people developed a proper attitude to God. So he made them destroy their Canaanite idols, and then organized a national assembly at Mizpah. As he prayed and offered sacrifices, the Philistines gathered to attack the worshipping crowds. At last the longed-for miracle happened, and the Philistines were routed at Ebenezer.

But Samuel's own satisfaction at seeing the worship of Yahweh restored to Israel was short-lived. Like Eli before him, he suffered the sadness of seeing his own two sons turn their back on his example and his faith. It became obvious that they could not succeed him in judging Israel when he died. The people began to look more closely at the organization of the surrounding nations. And they decided that they wanted a king just like the other nations. His power would not be limited to a small locality or short period of time, as that of the judges had usually been. They needed a leader in peacetime as well as war.

1 Samuel 8:4-22

Samuel was not enthusiastic at first. He saw behind the request a rejection of God's kingship. He warned Israel of the very high demands a king would make on the nation. He warned them of conscription to the army, of forced labour on the king's land and in his court, of taxes imposed on everyone. But their minds were made up. Samuel must find them a king.

And once more, a man was taken from an insignificant place and job and elevated to the position of national hero.

Israel's first king

Saul, a young man from the small tribe of Benjamin, had lost some of his father's donkeys which he had been looking after. For several days he and a companion searched for them in vain. In desperation they went to the house of Samuel the prophet, hoping he would be able to tell them where the animals were. Samuel was indeed able to tell the men where to find them, but he had a bigger surprise in store for Saul.

He invited Saul to a dinner party, then, convinced that this was the person chosen by God to be the first king of Israel, privately anointed his head with oil as a sign that he should be king.

The act of anointing was significant. In the Fertile Crescent the anointing of kings was rare. The Pharaohs of Egypt were never anointed with oil, but, if a Pharaoh wanted to appoint someone to rule for him over part of Palestine or Syria, then this assistant king would be anointed to show that he was under the control of the Pharaoh. All the kings of Israel were anointed to show that they were ruling under the control of God who was the true king of Israel.

Soon after he had been anointed, Saul was called by Samuel to meet all the people at Mizpah, and in their cry, 'Long live the king' the nation accepted him as their ruler. Saul did not have to wait long to prove himself worthy of the title. When the town of Jabesh-Gilead was besieged and threatened by Nahash, the cruel king of the Ammonites, he rallied the tribes together, marched on the enemy, and defeated them. This victory convinced Israel that Saul, like the judges before him, had been chosen by God. They went to Gilgal to confirm him as king in a religious ceremony.

1 Samuel 10:24

1 Samuel 11

The conflict with the Philistines, which had begun in the time of the judges when these sea peoples had invaded Canaan, continued sporadically. Saul's son, Jonathan, helped win an important battle with them at Michmash, sending them running away in disorder. But still they were not totally defeated, and they posed a constant threat to Israel. They had at least been ejected from the inland, if not from the coastal areas, and Saul's army was now able to move more easily up and down the country. And for the first time since Joshua divided the land among the tribes, Israel faced the enemy as a united nation. As a result of this the Philistines were forced to flee in disorder.

1 Samuel 14

Saul was not like many kings. He had no splendid palace or highly-organized civil service and lived fairly simply at his home in Gibeah. There was a small regular army; Saul could never have coped if he had relied solely on recruiting the soldiers from tribes each time there was an attack. Although Saul never actually led all Israel into battle, he came closer to it than any of the judges before him. He was a popular hero and his reign began well. Everything seemed set for a successful future.

Saul's downfall

But Saul, a good-looking, brave and generous man, had a darker side to his character. He had a very fiery temper and an unstable personality that was to cause his downfall. As Saul's responsibilities for the kingdom grew he alternated between clear-headed leadership, and violence and depression. Even members of his own family found him almost impossible to live with.

His problems were made worse by two other facts. He had been unable to deal a final knockout blow to the Philistines and thus ensure peace for Israel. And now that the tribes enjoyed their independence, Saul found it much harder to control them and keep the nation united.

1 Samuel 13:8-15

But, worst of all, he quarrelled with Samuel. When Saul tried to take over some of Samuel's priestly duties before one of the important battles, the quarrel between them became very serious indeed. Samuel told Saul that God had rejected him from being king because he had disobeyed God. Saul felt that his power was waning and his depression became worse. At times he would lash out wildly at any who came near him. Only music could calm him and David, who was to become his successor, was introduced into the court as a minstrel whose songs often soothed the raging king.

Saul and David

1 Samuel 16:13

From this point the Bible narrative focuses on David, the eighth son of Jesse from Bethlehem, and a member of the tribe of Judah. He was still only a shepherd boy when anointed by Samuel as king in place of Saul, who was still alive and ruling Israel. Only later was David the minstrel introduced into Saul's court. When Saul was in one of his black moods he probably never noticed who was playing the harp to him.

David became popular at the court and Saul's son Jonathan was his closest friend. This friendship was to last all their lives. But Saul became increasingly suspicious of David. He felt that the people saw God at work in David's life, and probably thought that they would prefer this young man as their king.

1 Samuel 19:8-17

Saul's jealousy reached such a pitch that eventually David was forced to become an outlaw to escape from the king's anger and attempts on his life.

1 Samuel 31

Saul's life came to a tragic end within four years of forcing David to become an outlaw. He was defeated by his old enemies, the Philistines, at the foot of Mt Gilboa. It was a desperate attempt to reassert his authority, but it failed, and Saul died on the mountain together with Jonathan and two of his other sons.

We cannot be certain about the length of Saul's reign. The Bible does not give precise dating and scholars have suggested anything from two to forty years! However, he must have been in power for some considerable time because he came to the throne while he was still a young man and shortly

2 Samuel 2:8

after his death his youngest son, Ishbosheth, became king when he was forty years old. Saul probably ruled for between twenty and thirty years.

When Saul died, Israel was left at the mercy of the Philistines again and they reoccupied as much land as they had possessed before Saul came to power. The condition of Israel seemed hopeless once again, yet within a few years it became one of the leading nations of Palestine and Syria, due largely to its most famous king, David.

Hero and outlaw

David was the youngest of a large family. Jesse, his father, was an important but not very wealthy man in the small town of Bethlehem. He was quite unimportant within the tribe of Judah to which he belonged, however.

David had a tough childhood. From an early age he was a shepherd in the roughest part of the country. Often his life would have been threatened by both wild beasts and wild men attacking the flocks. Yet this boy, to his family's surprise, was chosen to become the king to succeed Saul.

David, first introduced to Saul's court as a musician, became

1 Samuel 17:31-49

more widely known after killing Goliath. The giant Philistine had frightened the Israelite army into submission, but was killed by a stone from David's sling. From then on David proved himself to be a brave soldier and rapidly gained promotion. He struck up a close friendship with Saul's son

1 Samuel 18:20-29

Jonathan, married Saul's daughter Michal and quickly became one of the most popular men in Israel. But Saul, during fits of jealousy, made several attempts to kill David. Attempts were made to reconcile the two men, but without success. David became the leader of a band of outlaws, always trying to keep one jump ahead of the angry Saul who from time to time tried to hunt them down.

Above: sheep are often looked after by children in the Near East. David learned resourcefulness while caring for his father's flocks.

Above right: David frequently hid from Saul in caves in the Judean hills. This freshwater stream at Engedi, near the Dead Sea, is known as 'David's Spring'.

During the time that he was an outlaw, David went out of his way to make friends with the leaders of the tribe of Judah. He knew that their support would be of value later. Immediately after Saul's death it was in fact these men who chose David to be their king, and he set up his court at Hebron in Judah. David no doubt hoped that his popularity would win over the tribes in the north as well. However, Abner, one of Saul's leading followers and also his cousin, promptly made Saul's remaining son Ishbosheth king of the northern tribes. This probably pleased the Philistines because a divided Israel would be weaker and less able to resist their assaults.

For a while there were border skirmishes between the two rival kingdoms but when Ishbosheth quarrelled with Abner

2 Samuel 3,4

the end was near. Abner changed sides to join David and two of Ishbosheth's army captains killed their now defenceless king, thereby hoping to win David's favour. But instead of a reward they were executed by David for their disloyalty. After this the tribes of the north invited David to reign over them. The nation of Israel was united once more.

The kingdom united

The first thing David had to do after taking over the whole nation was to crush a Philistine threat to the new kingdom. Then he set about taking the Jebusite fortress of Jerusalem. It was a strong city, but Joab, David's cousin and a battle-hero, entered it by leading a party of soldiers up the underground shaft supplying water to the city. The shaft ran from a cave 40 feet/13 metres beneath the surface and the Jebusites never believed that anyone would try to enter the city by this route. But once Joab and his soldiers were in the city the strong fortress was useless. Jerusalem was at last in Israelite hands.

From that moment the fort was called the City of David and became the capital of the Israelite kingdom. David built a palace as his headquarters and then brought the ark of the covenant into the city. By these two acts he created both a political and a religious centre.

2 Samuel 8

David was not content simply to unite the twelve tribes of Israel into one nation. The greater part of his thirty-three years as king was spent in enlarging his empire and making it secure. When he died, Phoenicia, the country next to Israel on the Mediterranean coast, was linked to it by friendship and trade treaties. David also controlled the land from the River Euphrates in the east to the borders of Philistia and Sinai in the south. It was a large kingdom for those days, and some of his success was due to the fact that both Egypt and the

Government and religion under King David

David led the government himself, and built up a much more elaborate system than had existed during the time of Saul. He appointed Joab as commander-in-chief of the army, and the chief priests Zadok and Abiathar looked after matters of religion.

Taxes were probably imposed on the countries which David had conquered. He also held a census among his own people which may have been intended as a basis for taxing them, as well as to determine the strength of his manpower. But whatever the reason, the act met with the disapproval of David's advisers, and, eventually, his own conscience as well.

David seems to have taken very little active part in the administration of justice. Matters of law and order were probably dealt with at a tribal level, but there was a growing need for a national system of justice.

However, David did take considerable interest in Israel's religion. He was a devout man, who developed Jerusalem as the national religious centre. He hoped one day to be able to build a temple there, where the ark of the covenant could be kept. In fact he went so far as to draw up plans for it. He befriended Hiram, king of Tyre, hoping that he would provide advisers and timber for the building. But he was unable to begin the project; the Bible suggests that it was because he was a man of war

and to build the temple would have been hypocritical. It was left to Solomon, who was no soldier, to do it instead.

The music used in the worship in Jerusalem owed much to David's interest and influence. He was an accomplished musician, who had first been introduced to Saul's court as a harpist to soothe the king's tormented mind. It is likely that a number of the psalms which were used in worship had been composed by David, and are among those collected in the Book of Psalms in the Bible. The inclusion of music and song in worship was nothing new or unusual. In Mesopotamia about the time of Abraham music had been used in religious meetings, and collections of hymns have been discovered.

Mesopotamian peoples were too weak to stop his invasions.

The closing years of David's reign were marred by two serious revolts. One was within his own family and was led by his favourite son, Absalom. It began shortly after Absalom had been sent into exile from the court of David for murdering his brother. David's general, Joab, had done much to restore the boy's status and on his return Absalom tried to win the affections and support of the people. He spent four years preparing his plan and then one day went to Hebron, David's old capital, and had himself made king. He raised an army and set out to capture Jerusalem. Absalom pursued David from the city as he fled for his life, but the revolutionary army was defeated. Absalom was killed by Joab in spite of David's clear order that he should be kept alive.

2 Samuel 14-18

The second revolt took place when David was very old and not expected to live for long. Adonijah, the eldest of his sons, tried to seize the throne and had himself proclaimed king. He was supported by Joab and a priest called Abiathar. The news was brought to David by Bathsheba, whom he had married some years before after deliberately sending her husband to the battlefront where he was killed. The dying king ordered that Solomon be placed on David's mule and anointed king by Zadok the priest. When news reached Adonijah he fled for safety to the altar in the temple, a place where traditionally no one could be killed, until the new king, Solomon, promised that his life should be spared. So David died, happy in the knowledge that Solomon, the son of his choice, was to be the next king.

1 Kings 1

2 Samuel 11

'Solomon's Pools' near Bethlehem are connected with King Solomon by tradition. They probably date from Roman times and were reservoirs supplying Jerusalem with water by gravity flow.

Solomon: builder and merchant

King Solomon was famous above all for building the temple. This great building, which was set up in Jerusalem on the site that David had bought years before, was Solomon's most outstanding work from a lifetime of building.

When he became king he executed all those who had supported Adonijah's attempt to win the kingdom. Adonijah himself had been promised his life as long as he never again interfered in state affairs. When he broke this condition, Solomon had him executed as well.

Unlike his father, Solomon was no soldier. His task was not to build the empire, but to hold it together. He fought no important battles, but tried to maintain friendly relationships

1 Kings 11:1-4

inside the empire and with neighbouring nations. To develop these relations Solomon married numerous princesses of neighbouring states, no doubt hoping that the kings would not attack if their daughters were living in Solomon's territory! His most important marriage was to an Egyptian princess and when she came to Jerusalem it was to much luxury and extra-

1 Kings 11:9-14

special treatment. But the women brought their religions with them, and when he was an old man Solomon worshipped other gods besides Yahweh.

1 Kings 9:15-19

In another attempt to keep the empire safe, Solomon fortified such cities as Hazor, Megiddo, Gezer, Beth-horon and Tamar. In the first three, archaeologists have found a uniform style of gateways dating from Solomon's time. Troops stationed in these cities could easily be called upon for quick defence against enemies from outside the empire as well as for peace-keeping at home.

All this cost money. Solomon soon realized that his income had not kept pace with the building costs and the costs of running the empire. But he was a master of trade and industry. Israel lay across the great trade routes from Egypt and Arabia

1 Kings 10:1-13

into Cilicia (modern Turkey) and beyond. The Queen of Sheba may have come to visit Solomon to discuss trade matters in which they were both competing, as well as to test his famous wisdom.

With the help of shipbuilders from Phoenicia, Solomon built a fleet of trading ships at Ezion-geber. Phoenician sailors manned the ships and they brought Solomon supplies of gold, silver, rare timber, ivory and even monkeys – probably to entertain the members of Solomon's court.

Ezion-geber was also famous for Solomon's copper industry. Copper was mined in the Arabah nearby, and the furnaces were built to make use of the strong northerly winds which fanned the flames to the high temperatures needed to melt the ore. Solomon had as much copper as he needed for his own use and a good deal more for export.

The Egyptians needed good horses for their chariots and again Solomon was able to turn this to his advantage. He bought horses from Cilicia and sold them at a large profit to

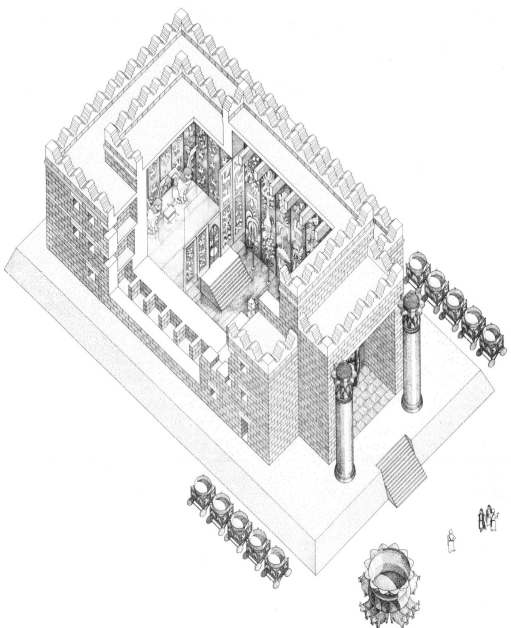

Solomon's temple

Solomon had been king for four years when he began work on the Jerusalem temple and it took seven years to build. He had renewed the treaty of friendship that David had set up with Hiram, king of Tyre, and from him Solomon was able to employ good architects. From the Lebanon mountains within Hiram's territory came the famous cedar trees used for the woodwork. Great rafts of timber were floated down the coast from Tyre to Israel and then dragged across country to Jerusalem. Stone was cut from the hills of Judah. The carved wood panelling inside was covered in gold, and copper was used to make this a spectacular building. The temple itself was rectangular in shape and had the same two main 'rooms' as the tent of meeting which Moses had built.

the Egyptians. The centre of his horse trade was the town of Megiddo, where in recent times the ancient ruins of some stables have been found. In spite of all this, Solomon still could not make ends meet. So he was forced to take drastic steps to deal with the problem.

1 Kings 4:7-19
First, he laid heavy taxes on his people and to make collection easier he divided the country into twelve districts. Each district had its own governor who was responsible to the king, but these districts were not the same as the old tribal districts and this caused a good deal of unrest. Each district was expected to provide food for one month each year to be sent to the king and his court at Jerusalem.

1 Kings 5:13-18
In the second place, Solomon did something that made the Israelites hate him even more. He began a system of forced labour. Every able-bodied man was expected to work for the king without pay for three months each year. True, Solomon started with non-Israelite labour, but when he began to call on the services of the Israelites themselves he was accused of

1 Samuel 8:10-18
breaking God's covenant. Some of Samuel's prophecies about the ways a king would rule were beginning to come true.

Solomon's reign had its splendid moments. But he overburdened his people, and when he died the empire soon fell apart.

Trade in Solomon's time

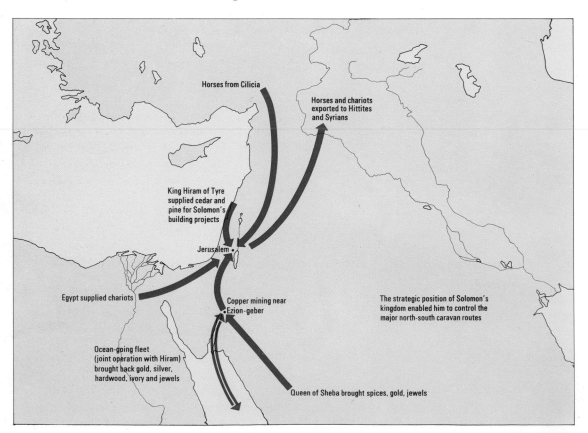

Horses from Cilicia

Horses and chariots exported to Hittites and Syrians

King Hiram of Tyre supplied cedar and pine for Solomon's building projects

Jerusalem •

Egypt supplied chariots

Copper mining near • Ezion-geber

The strategic position of Solomon's kingdom enabled him to control the major north-south caravan routes

Ocean-going fleet (joint operation with Hiram) brought back gold, silver, hardwood, ivory and jewels

Queen of Sheba brought spices, gold, jewels

The kingdom divided

The kings of Israel were expected to rule in obedience to God. They were also expected to unite the twelve tribes into one nation. Solomon failed in both these tasks. He had tried to be too much the powerful ruler and not enough the servant. He had neglected the worship of God and had turned to some of the gods of surrounding nations. The heavy taxes which he put on his people together with plans for forced labour turned many against him.

The first three kings of Israel had come from southern tribes. Saul was from the tribe of Benjamin and David and Solomon from Judah. The northern tribes felt that the south had been shown too much favouritism, and Solomon's attitude and actions made the family of David even more unpopular.

1 Kings 11:26-40 During his reign there had been one attempt by the northern tribes to rebel, but Solomon had been able to squash it. A prophet called Ahijah had foretold that all except one tribe would be taken from Solomon's family as a punishment for his excesses. The leader of the uprising, Jeroboam, went into exile in Egypt after his defeat, as Solomon continued to try to kill him. There he waited, and when Solomon died, Jeroboam returned to lead the north.

A fatal decision

933 BC

When Solomon's son, Rehoboam, took over the throne from his father, trouble began at once. He had been accepted as king without question by the tribes in the south, but that was not enough. To rule *all* Israel Rehoboam had to win the goodwill of the northern tribes as well. So he went to Shechem to be proclaimed king by the north.

1 Kings 12:1-16 Here he was met by Jeroboam who, on behalf of the north, demanded a reduction in taxes and the end of forced labour. Foolishly, Rehoboam rejected the advice of the older and more experienced statesmen who had served his father Solomon. They told him to agree to what in the circumstances was a very reasonable request. Instead, he turned to his younger advisers and accepted their suggestion that Rehoboam should make even harsher demands on the northern tribes. Had Rehoboam accepted the advice of the older men, he might have saved the nation. Instead, he caused a division in the kingdom that was never healed.

The northern tribes turned their backs on the family of David and refused union with the south. They then set up a new kingdom which they called Israel. It was made up of ten of the twelve tribes and Jeroboam was elected to be their first king. Rehoboam was left with two tribes only, Judah and Benjamin. Together they made up the smaller of the two Israelite kingdoms and took the name Judah, after the larger of the tribes.

The most immediate – and serious – results of this division of the kingdom was that the old empire of David and Solomon, which had dominated a wide area and many nations, disappeared almost overnight. Neither Judah nor Israel was powerful enough, on its own, to keep the empire together. The nations that had paid taxes to Israel took advantage of the situation and stopped sending the money, knowing that neither kingdom could force them to pay. Solomon's big commercial and industrial enterprises ended and border fighting broke out between north and south. Israel and Judah both became second-rate nations in the Near East.

Rehoboam: 930–913 BC (Judah) Rehoboam probably realized that it was useless trying to make Israel return to him. Most of the army was in the north and those soldiers who were still in Judah were too few to be of much use, even if they had wanted to fight.

1 Kings 14:25-28 If he had ever hoped for reunion with Israel that hope disappeared when Egypt invaded both nations. The Bible concentrates on the attack on Judah, but Egyptian records, still preserved today, show that the invasion went right through Palestine. It was led by Pharaoh Shishak in about 925 BC. He intended to restore Egyptian power in Palestine and Syria, but he was unsuccessful because of problems within Egypt itself. Judah had been damaged by this invasion; many of the temple treasures were plundered by the invaders. Rehoboam was left so weak that he could do little more than keep his own people safe from further attacks. There was now no chance of regaining – and re-uniting – Israel.

Jeroboam I: 930–910 BC (Israel) Jeroboam had the difficult task of trying to create a new nation where there had been none before. He had no capital city, no proper organization for state affairs and no religious centre.

He began by creating a new capital at Shechem; a few years later, he moved the capital to Tirzah about seven miles away. But the real problem was the religious one. Deep in the hearts of the Israelites was the belief that God had saved his people from Egypt and given them a covenant which was to rule their lives. They had seen how David had made Jerusalem the religious centre of the nation and many still felt that they ought to be loyal to the worship of God in the temple there. But Jerusalem was Rehoboam's capital and they had rejected Rehoboam and all that he stood for.

If Jeroboam allowed his people to go to Jerusalem to worship, then he might lose them altogether. The worshippers could easily have been attracted to the Davidic family. That would have been a disaster for Jeroboam. To try to solve his

The divided kingdom

David made Jerusalem the capital of a united Israel. Even when the kingdom split, many of the tribes ruled by Jeroboam from a new capital still looked to Jerusalem as their spiritual home.

problem, he built two shrines or small temples to rival the great temple in Jerusalem, one at Bethel in the south of Israel and the other at Dan in the north.

In both shrines he put an image of a bull, perhaps designed to act as a kind of platform on which the invisible God, Yahweh, was to have his throne. But the bulls were very like those the Canaanites actually put their idols on. Jeroboam had opened the way for his people to return to the Canaanite religion which had been outlawed by Moses and the judges. The authors of the books of Kings in the Bible looked back to Jeroboam as the king 'who caused Israel to sin' by re-introducing idol worship.

Of the two kingdoms, Judah was the weaker. But it lasted longer than Israel, and during the next 340 years remained loyal to the family of David with one of his descendants always occupying the throne. Israel, on the other hand, was much less stable. It had nineteen kings during 212 stormy years. Of these kings, nine took the throne by force, seven were murdered, and one committed suicide.

Prophets and politics

With the disintegration of the kingdom came a decline in the calibre of the kings. The example of political wisdom and religious faithfulness set by David – despite his occasional lapses – was not often followed by his successors in either north or south. Their religious compromise was, to the biblical historians, the cause of most regret. But into the situation came a succession of religious leaders – prophets – who took the kings to task for abandoning the ancient laws and commandments. The conflict between prophets and politicians was often bitter, and none more so than that between Elijah and Ahab, king of the northern state of Israel.

Elijah denounces idolatry

Omri: 885–874 BC (Israel)

After Jeroboam's death in 910 BC, the northern kingdom had been torn apart by civil war for thirty-four years. Then one of the army commanders, Omri, became king. He built a new capital city at Samaria, fortifying it so well that in later times it withstood several sieges. He made friends with Phoenicia and so renewed the old contract that David and Solomon had begun. He then arranged for his son, Ahab, to marry Jezebel, the daughter of Ethbaal, king of Tyre, the main city of Phoenicia. The move proved disastrous for Israel as Jezebel insisted on bringing her religion to Israel. This precipitated an inevitable clash with the prophet Elijah.

Omri's new capital city of Samaria occupied an easily-defended hilltop site and later became a centre of idol-worship under King Ahab. This is a modern Samaritan village built on terraced slopes, near the ancient capital.

It was, of course, quite normal for a foreign princess to be allowed to practise her religion in the country to which she moved on her marriage. But Jezebel was not content to worship her god Melkart quietly. She was so full of enthusiasm for her religion that she wanted to impose it on Israel. Phoenicia was a very powerful nation at that time, so Ahab was expected to show great respect to this new god, and when he became king, he built a shrine for it at Samaria. If Jezebel had been allowed to have her own way, the worship of Yahweh would have been completely removed from Israel.

Melkart was the Phoenician name for the old Canaanite god Baal, and Jezebel was, therefore, reviving the old religion of Canaan in Israel. Some protest was made, but many of those who did complain were put to death. Elijah, however, escaped such a fate, and emerged as a rugged and powerful opponent of the queen and her husband. Elijah lived in Gilead and appeared suddenly and unannounced in Israel. Nothing is known about his home or family.

He wanted to remind Israel of the great exodus from Egypt and of God's covenant with them. Obedience to this covenant, he said, had always been the best rule of life and he longed to see the people return to it. He was God's champion and wanted to show how powerless the god of Jezebel was. He began by promising that there would be a drought and subsequent famine for three years as a sign of God's judgement. Melkart would no doubt be expected by his worshippers to prevent the famine, but it happened as Elijah predicted.

1 Kings 17:2

At the end of the three years Elijah returned again to lead the people back to the worship of God. He challenged the followers and prophets of Melkart to a contest on Mt Carmel. They built altars for sacrifice and agreed that only the one who was truly God in Israel could produce fire from heaven to burn up the offering. The utter failure of the prophets of Melkart to get their god to hear and answer was matched by Elijah's spectacular success in the name of Yahweh. This was followed by rain bringing the drought to an end. Yet in spite of this impressive event, little seems to have been achieved. Elijah's life was threatened by the angry Jezebel and he fled for safety to Mt Sinai.

1 Kings 18:17-40

1 Kings 19:1-18

While this was happening in Israel, Ahab was having to deal with a threat from Syria. Even in his father Omri's day Syria had been often at war with Israel and Judah, in an attempt to control the roads to Egypt and Arabia. The ruler of Syria at this time was Benhadad and about 855 BC he attacked Samaria, the capital of Israel. The attack failed and in the following year Benhadad was so badly beaten by Ahab's army that he had to beg for peace. He was forced to return the cities that Syria had once taken from Israel, but when peace was granted by Ahab it lasted only for three years.

1 Kings 20:26-34

The Assyrians

The Assyrians were a Semitic people, occupying an area which is now in northern Iraq. Records show that they were living in their land around 2300 BC and that their language closely resembled Babylonian.

Assyria became a leading nation in the Near East between 1500 and 1100 BC and ruled as far west as the River Euphrates. A period of recession and chaos followed this as Aramaean nomads raided Assyria and considerably reduced its power. From about 900 BC onwards, a succession of warrior-kings set about regaining lost territory and establishing firm control over the expanding empire.

The Bible frequently mentions the Assyrians, who were an almost constant threat to Israel and Judah from about 750 BC onwards. When they defeated a nation, the Assyrians often deported most of the population to other parts of the empire to lessen the risk of any resistance. They then replaced them with foreigners. They also demanded taxes (or 'tribute') from conquered states, a practice which gave rise to repeated rebellions.

Right: King Jehu of Israel was one of the rulers who was forced to pay tribute to Assyria. The 'Black Obelisk' was discovered in 1846 at Nimrud, about 25 miles/40km south of Nineveh, where Shalmaneser III (858–824 BC) had his palace. It is a black limestone pillar, about 6½ feet/2m high, and has five carved panels on each of its four sides. The second panel from the top depicts Jehu prostrate before King Shalmaneser and is the only known portrayal of an Israelite king.

The expansion of the Assyrian Empire

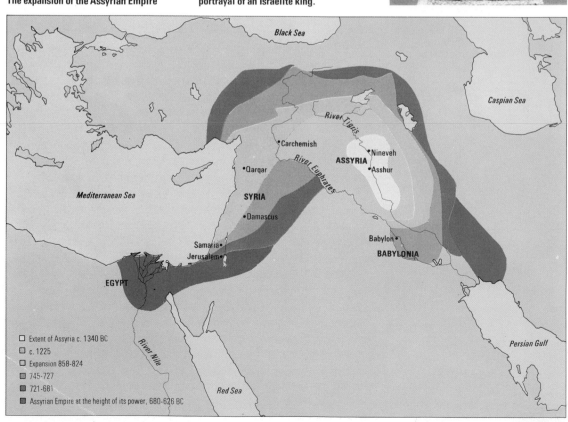

Extent of Assyria c. 1340 BC
c. 1225
Expansion 858-824
745-727
721-681
Assyrian Empire at the height of its power, 680-626 BC

Top: King Ashurbanipal (669–627 BC) and his queen are pictured feasting in their garden, with servants and musicians in attendance. The Assyrian Empire was at its largest extent during the reigns of Esarhaddon (681–669 BC) and Ashurbanipal. In fact, it became too large to be effectively controlled or defended.

Above: Many Assyrian reliefs depict scenes of siege and warfare. These panels are from Sennacherib's palace at Nineveh and are part of a large frieze showing the siege at Lachish. During the reign of King Hezekiah of Judah, the Assyrian king Sennacherib (705–681 BC) 'attacked the fortified cities of Judah and conquered them' (2 Kings 18:13); Lachish, about 25 miles/40km south-west of Jerusalem, was almost certainly one of these cities. In the centre of the relief, Sennacherib is seen seated on his throne receiving booty taken from the city, while the conquered inhabitants kneel before him. The royal tent is pitched on a wooded slope behind the king.

Above: Sennacherib ordered that accounts of his military campaigns should be recorded on hexagonal clay prisms. This prism gives Sennacherib's own account, in boastful language, of his siege of Jerusalem and his conquests of numerous settlements in Judah. The biblical narrative describes the dramatic salvation of Jerusalem from the Assyrian attackers.

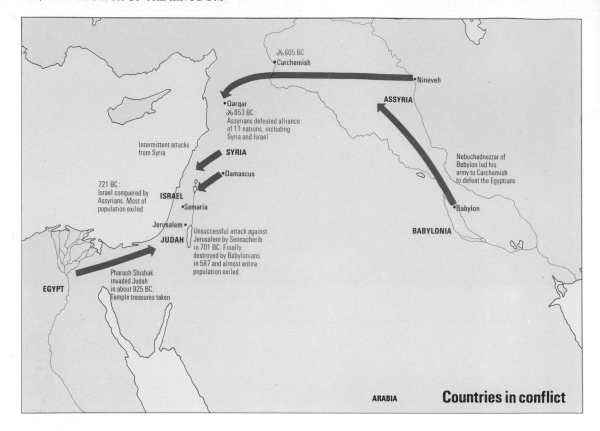

Countries in conflict

Threats from Assyria

1 Kings 22:29-36

Jehu: 841–813 BC (Israel)

It was during those three years that a growing power, Assyria, began to make itself felt in northern Mesopotamia. Noted for their extreme cruelty, the Assyrians presented a very real threat to both Syria and Israel. As a result, Ahab and Benhadad forgot their own quarrels and together with another ten kings formed a league to resist Assyria.

The league met the armies of Assyria at Qarqar on the River Orontes in Syria in 853 BC. Shalmaneser III, the king of Assyria, claimed a great victory at the battle, but it may well have been inconclusive, with neither side gaining any advantage. He did not follow up his victory and in fact returned home leaving the whole region in peace for many years.

After the battle of Qarqar, Ahab and Benhadad were soon fighting one another again and Ahab was killed in 850 BC at the Battle of Ramoth-Gilead. The whole of the family of Omri and Ahab was finally destroyed some years later by a new king of Israel, Jehu. The massacre was part of his successful campaign to remove all traces of Baal worship from Israel. He did have to submit to Syria and Assyria, however, and was forced to pay tribute to Shalmaneser III.

From about 850 BC there were nearly fifty years of peace for the kingdom of Israel. Syria had been badly defeated by Assyria which itself was so troubled by internal affairs that it gave no attention to Israel. During this time Israel was able to

Jeroboam II: 782–745 BC (Israel)

regain some of its prosperity under the leadership of Jeroboam II who won back the lands previously lost to Syria. Life became more settled and the future looked hopeful once again. But the wealth was in the hands of too few people, most of whom were merchants. The peasants, who had for many years been the backbone of Israelite life, were almost completely ignored, and continued to live from hand to mouth.

Amos and social justice

Into this situation came another prophet, Amos, in about 750 BC. Amos was a southerner from Tekoa, a town about 6 miles/ 10km south of Bethlehem in the kingdom of Judah, but his preaching was directed towards the north. Tekoa lay near the main road running up the centre of the country and passing through major towns including Beersheba, Hebron and Jerusalem. Living in such a place, Amos was well aware of the events in the world around. His life as a shepherd was not easy, but his work probably brought him into the main market towns where he sold his sheep.

Amos was prompted to speak out against dishonesty and hypocrisy by what he saw in the market-places.

Amos 5:10-12; 6:1-7; 8:4-6

Amos saw fraudulent deals in the markets, poor people being sold as slaves and judges accepting bribes. The rich people lived in the lap of luxury, and were unwilling to lift a finger to help the poor. In the face of all this corruption Amos believed God had called him to speak to the people. He reminded them of the deliverance from Egypt and the goodness of God. He called them to remember the covenant, and put it into practice.

Amos 5:21-24

Amos saw that the people were attending the religious services regularly, but what amazed him was that their worship seemed so insincere. It should have made them more concerned than they evidently were for right personal living

Who were the prophets?

From the time of the judges onwards, a group of men took an ever increasingly important place in the history of the Hebrews. They were the prophets. Moses had been regarded as the first prophet, but it was not until Israel had settled in Canaan that prophets became more numerous.

They appeared mainly in times of national crisis as God's spokesmen. Their message placed particular emphasis on two issues. First, they taught that a special relationship existed between the Hebrews and God. See Amos 3:1-2 and Hosea 11:1-2, for instance. Second, God expected his people to live morally upright lives. Nathan the prophet confronted David over the way the king had organized the death of Bathsheba's husband in 2 Samuel 12:1-15.

Several terms are used in the Old Testament to describe the prophets:
Man of God. In 1 Samuel 2:27 the old man Eli is visited by a 'man of God' who tells him about the bad behaviour of Eli's two sons.
Seer. These men claimed to *see* God's plans for the world and to *see* into human affairs. Saul consulted Samuel as a 'seer' when he wanted to find his lost donkeys (1 Samuel 9).
Prophet. This is a term which can have two meanings. It can refer to someone who *is called* or to someone who *calls or speaks*. It is probably right to link both these ideas together; a prophet was a

man who felt himself called by God for the special task of speaking God's message to God's people.

The prophets then, were first and foremost men with the message of God. They called people to turn away from unhelpful and wrong ways of living and return to live in harmony with God and with their fellow-men. They often fearlessly denounced political and social corruption and religious practices associated with foreign gods.

The message of the prophets came, they insisted, because they were living in a close relationship with God and had therefore been admitted into God's secret plans. God was seen as the controller of history and the prophets claimed to interpret history correctly. So they looked back to the past in order to remind the Israelites of the way in which God had chosen them for himself and to urge them to have faith again in him.

They also examined the present to show how the situation in which people were living could be understood in the light of the character of God. In effect, they were saying, 'Because God is loving and just, then he expects you to live in loving and just ways now.'

The prophets also looked towards the future. They taught that God would continue to keep his promises to Israel and bring the nation through difficult times, and by means of discipline, into a brighter future in which God's rule would be established on the earth. This future was sometimes known as 'the day of the Lord', when God's judgement would be preceded by calamities such as earthquakes and political turmoil. The last prophet of this kind to be mentioned in the Bible is John the Baptizer, a cousin of Jesus. He had the special task of preparing people for Jesus' message.

In the New Testament church every member was encouraged to desire the gift of prophecy, as in 1 Corinthians 14:1. This would have been similar to, but not identical with, modern preaching. Instead of presenting a carefully-prepared sermon to the listeners, the prophet would speak spontaneously some message he believed came directly from God.

There seems to have been a special group of 'prophets' in the church as well. Their work was generally that of teaching and encouraging Christians to persevere with their new-found faith.

An idolatrous shrine was set up on Mt Tabor in Hosea's time.

and social relationships. Because Israel had broken the covenant, Amos could see that the future was not going to be bright. As a builder puts a plumb-line against a wall while it is being built to make sure that it rises straight, so, said Amos, God had put his plumb-line, the covenant, against Israel and found that the nation was crooked. The only possible outcome of this was judgement, and Amos saw it coming as an invasion from Assyria and the removal of Israel from the land.

Amos 7:7-9

No one took his message seriously. Life seemed good and preaching like his was not welcome in Israel. He was forced to leave Israel in disgrace, but though his words were ignored Amos believed that God had spoken through him. His message was written down, however, and his book is now in the Old Testament.

Amos 7:12-13

After about thirty years Amos' warning came true. In 721 BC the Assyrians, under their king Sargon II, conquered Israel, and Samaria was captured and destroyed. Israel became the Assyrian province of Samaria and the tribes were scattered. Only a few people remained, and the land was left desolate. It was not the purpose of Sargon to leave the conquered land unoccupied, however, so he sent exiles from other lands to live there. These intermarried with the remnant of the Israelite population and from them came the mixed race called the Samaritans. Jews from the south never recognized Samaritans as true Israelites and in Jesus' day they would have no contact with them.

John 4:9

Peace in Judah

Unlike Israel, the smaller nation of Judah enjoyed some years of relative peace after the division of the kingdoms about 930 BC. Members of David's family succeeded to the throne except for one brief period between 841 and 835 BC when Athaliah, a daughter of Ahab and widow of one of the kings of Judah, seized it for herself. This was the only break with the line of David and, for the most part, life in Judah was less dramatic than in Israel.

The wealth of Judah increased considerably during the reign of Uzziah although, as in Israel, most of it belonged to a minority of people. Uzziah began a building programme and re-opened the copper-smelting furnaces at Ezion-geber. Farming, too, was improved in the south of the land. The year Uzziah died, a man named Isaiah had a vision of God in the temple at Jerusalem in which he was called to bring God's message to the people of Judah. He may have been a member of a noble family, and thus able to come easily into the king's presence. For fifty years he worked mainly in royal circles as a critic and adviser of kings.

791–740 BC

During the reign of Ahaz, Assyria grew more and more powerful. The three nations of Syria, Israel and Judah stood between Assyria and Egypt and seemed likely targets in the Assyrian programme of expansion. Syria and Israel wanted

735–715 BC

Judah to join them in resisting the pressure of Assyria. Ahaz refused their invitation, however, and so Israel and Syria threatened Judah with war in 734 BC. Ahaz was keen to turn to Assyria for help. Isaiah advised him not to panic, but to trust in God. The king did not take his advice.

The Assyrians certainly saved Judah from the clutches of Israel and Syria, but they demanded such a high price that Judah was almost crippled. The king had rejected the message from Isaiah in the interests of safety, but he paid dearly for it.

Hezekiah's Tunnel, about 600 yards/550m long, was built to secure Jerusalem's water-supply in times of siege. The tunnel winds its way from the Gihon Spring, shown here, to the Pool of Siloam. This was a major engineering achievement for its time and was constructed by two teams of workmen cutting through the rock from opposite ends. It is still possible to wade through the tunnel.

Hezekiah and the Assyrians

Isaiah again became involved in international politics during the reign of Hezekiah who succeeded Ahaz in 715 BC. Six years before, the northern kingdom of Israel had fallen to the might of Assyria. Hezekiah decided to reverse the policy of Ahaz and in 711 BC he began attempts to release his people from the powerful grip of Assyria.

Isaiah reminded Hezekiah that although it had been wrong to make foreign alliances, once they had been made, they ought to be kept. Egypt, hoping to be relieved of the Assyrian threat, encouraged Hezekiah to rebel. But, as Isaiah was quick to point out, no real help would come from Egypt. It was far too weak to play any big part in international affairs and in fact suffered a severe defeat at the hands of Assyria a few years later.

In 705 BC Hezekiah faced his biggest test when Sennacherib became king of Assyria. Judah, together with a number of other nations which had been paying tribute to Assyria, decided to pay no more. Sennacherib set out to deal with the rebels and in 701 BC reached Judah after successfully putting down the other revolts. It seemed obvious that Judah would fall, too. Forty-six cities were taken and more than 200,000 people made refugees. Jerusalem was in a state of siege.

Hezekiah pleaded for peace and Sennacherib agreed – at the price of all the gold and silver in the city. Again, Isaiah encouraged Hezekiah and the people to trust God to defend them as he had in the past. Their nerve wavered, but did not break, as the climax came. A force of Assyrian soldiers was sent to attack Jerusalem; Isaiah told Hezekiah that the city would not fall, and during the night Sennacherib's army was almost entirely wiped out. The Bible attributes the mysterious event to the angel of the Lord; the Jewish historian Josephus says it was due to a plague. The remaining Assyrians hurriedly withdrew from Judah. The tiny country had survived the onslaught of the most powerful empire of the time and Hezekiah ended his days in peace.

Hezekiah had reformed the religion of Judah very thoroughly during his lifetime, but after his death the nation slipped again into a period when God was largely forgotten. King Manasseh and King Amon allowed the religion of the Canaanites to flourish once more, a situation that was to last for about fifty years. Manasseh became king when he was only twelve years old and was the 'front' for a party of politicians opposed to Hezekiah's policies. His was a peaceful reign, but he encouraged heathen practices. Amon ruled for only two years before he was assassinated by members of his court. They replaced him with another boy-king, Amon's eight-year-old son Josiah.

2 Kings 18:13-18

2 Kings 18:19–19:37

The Book of Isaiah

The book of Isaiah contains some of the most memorable and important statements about God in the Old Testament. Its origin is a matter of some debate. There is little doubt that most of the first thirty-nine chapters come from the mouth of the prophet Isaiah who advised King Hezekiah during the Assyrian attacks. Chapters 36–39, for instance, consist largely of historical records of the invasion, and Hezekiah's response to it.

Chapters 40–66 are a different matter, however. Part of this section (40–55) deals with the exile of Judah in Babylon which was not to occur for some 150 years, and the rest addresses the Jews in Judah. For this reason many scholars have suggested that this part of the book was written by a later disciple of Isaiah. The book has always been known as a unity, however, and the New Testament authors refer to the various parts of the book as if they were all written by the same person.

But leaving aside the question of authorship, the book shows how Israel's conception of God had developed since Moses' time. It contains important teaching that is echoed in the New Testament.

Both sections of the book are preoccupied with the holiness of God and the sinfulness of people. Isaiah's prophetic ministry began with a vision, in the temple, of God's holiness and greatness (chapter 6). 'I am a man of unclean lips, and I dwell in the midst of a people of unclean lips; for my eyes have seen the king, the Lord of hosts. He frequently calls God 'the Holy One of Israel' (e.g. 12:6; 30:11, 12), who is angered by the disobedience of the nation but who is still faithful to his side of the covenant made with Moses.

In the later chapters come some of the most eloquent descriptions of God in the whole Bible, rivalling even the Psalms for beauty. God is seen as the almighty creator who continues to give life to his creatures (42:5). Compared with him 'the nations are like a drop from a bucket' (40:15), and any idol made by men is useless: 'If one cries to it, it does not answer or save him from trouble' (46:7).

But idolatry is not the only object of scorn in the book; so, too, is social injustice. Just as the southerner Amos had denounced the idle indulgence and injustice of the rich a generation earlier in the northern kingdom, Isaiah exposed the excessive luxury,

drunkenness and oppression in Judah (e.g. 3:14-26; 28:5-7).

Isaiah provides new insights into the Old Testament concept of the nation. He foresees a 'remnant' of people, a faithful minority, who will be the nucleus of a new nation which will once more serve God. At times he seems to have believed that the whole nation would be saved from punishment, as when the Assyrian king Sennacherib was miraculously driven back (38:35-37). But generally he saw only a small minority who would be saved from exile: 'And there will be a highway from Assyria for the remnant which is left of his people, as there was for Israel when they came up from the land of Egypt' (11:16).

Another unique element in the book comes in the second part, in four prophecies known as the 'servant songs' (42:1-4; 49:1-6; 50:4-9; 52:13–53:12). The servant appears to be first the nation itself, then a person who will save Israel from its enemies and who is a model of obedience to God. He is depicted as having humble origins, called by God and endowed with his Spirit to restore Israel from exile and give the knowledge of God to

non-Jews. He achieves this by his words, and although he works quietly and is innocent of wrong, others are violent towards him and eventually he is put to death for the sins of the nation.

It is not surprising that Christians have seen in these passages a clear foreshadowing of the life and sufferings of Jesus Christ, and the New Testament frequently quotes them.

Two other similar passages are also closely connected with Jesus. In chapter 11 (in a passage frequently read in Christmas carol services) there is a reference to a branch growing from the root of Jesse. Jesse was father of King David, and Jesus was descended from him. David was often regarded as the model king, and the hoped-for deliverer of Israel was expected to emulate David's faith and leadership.

In chapter 61 is the passage Jesus quoted in his first public address at the synagogue in Nazareth. Because he applied it to himself, some of his hearers tried to kill him for blasphemy: 'The Spirit of the Lord is upon me, because he has anointed me to preach good news to the poor.'

Isaiah compared the people of Judah to a vineyard which produced sour grapes: God expected them to do what was right but they continually rebelled against him.

Josiah's reforms

Josiah, like Manasseh, was surrounded with advisers. But this time most of them were true to Israel's traditional beliefs and practices. They encouraged Josiah to restore the worship of Yahweh to Judah. Money was collected and repairs were begun to bring the temple back into full use. Assyria had lost its grip on Palestine and was unlikely to make any attempt to stop the changes.

When the king had been on the throne for eighteen years a workman found a copy of the Book of the Law, as the temple repairs were nearing completion. This discovery gave a new impetus to Josiah's reforms. When he read the Book of the Law he saw just how far the nation had drifted from a true relationship to God. The book probably included a copy of Deuteronomy and perhaps parts of the other law books with which the Old Testament now begins.

623 BC

About the same time a young prophet called Jeremiah became convinced that God had commanded him to speak to the people of Judah. Jeremiah came from a priestly family, and lived at Anathoth, a village some 3 miles/5km north of Jerusalem. At first he was probably a strong supporter of the king's religious reforms. But he soon began to feel that they were not going far enough. There was plenty of organized worship, the law of God was being studied by the scribes, but these were merely the external acts of religion. Jeremiah felt that there had been no real return to the covenant and that most of the people still retained the old materialistic ways and superstition. There was little evidence that the people of Judah had recovered a close relationship with God.

Slowly but surely Jeremiah found himself preaching against the priests of Judah and even denouncing the temple re-organization. The people were not facing up to the implications of God's truth, claimed the prophet, and their worship was not wholehearted.

While Josiah's reforms were progressing within Judah, significant changes were taking place beyond its borders. The power of Assyria had dwindled so much that in 612 BC Nineveh fell and the old empire collapsed under the rising power of Babylon. To the south lay Egypt, which was beginning to assert itself once more. And between these two nations, each burning with ambition to expand its rule, lay the tiny kingdom of Judah. In a desperate attempt to help the Assyrians quell the Babylonian advance, Pharaoh Necho II marched north to Carchemish to confront the Babylonians in 609 BC.

2 Kings 23:28-30

Josiah heard of this move and set out with his own army to stop the Egyptians. He may well have seen Necho's activities as a threat to his own plans to unite Judah and Israel. But he was killed in battle at Megiddo. His son, Jehoiakim, was placed on the throne of Judah by the Egyptians and was expected to rule under their control. After this religious reforms simply died out. And when Necho was soundly routed by

Nebuchadnezzar's Babylonian troops, and chased back to his own country, Judah came under the jurisdiction of the new Babylonian Empire, and once again was forced to pay regular sums of 'tribute' money to the conquerors.

Rebellion at last broke out in Judah and in 598 BC the Babylonians marched to deal with the problem. They arrived to find that Jehoiakim had died and his son Jehoiachin was on the throne. He surrendered after three months' siege. Jerusalem was taken and the leading men of Judah were exiled to Babylon.

Jehoiachin's uncle, Zedekiah, replaced him as a puppet ruler obeying orders from Babylon. He was too weak to rule well, despite Jeremiah's encouragement, and when further rebellions broke out in 589 BC the Babylonians decided to make an example of Judah. Jerusalem was again taken and in 587 BC the city and the temple were destroyed and even more people taken hostage to Babylon. They included Zedekiah, who also suffered the punishment of being blinded for his unfaithfulness to his distant masters.

Jeremiah was given the opportunity to join the exiles, but he felt his place was to remain with the few poor people who had been left in Judah to cultivate the land. Eventually, these people forced him to go down with them into Egypt, where he probably died.

The Babylonian Empire

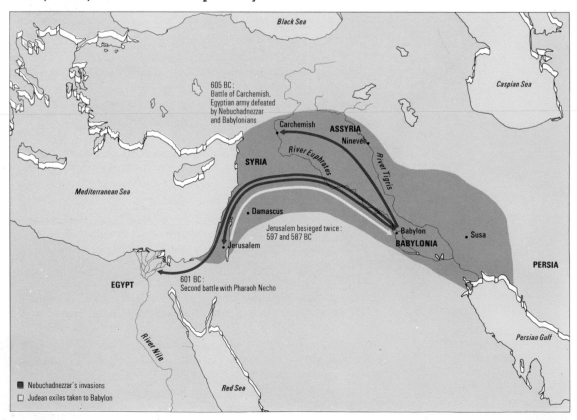

605 BC:
Battle of Carchemish.
Egyptian army defeated
by Nebuchadnezzar
and Babylonians

Black Sea

Caspian Sea

Carchemish   ASSYRIA
              Nineveh

River Euphrates   River Tigris

SYRIA

Mediterranean Sea

Damascus

Jerusalem besieged twice:
597 and 587 BC

Jerusalem   Babylon   Susa
                 BABYLONIA

PERSIA

EGYPT   601 BC:
         Second battle with Pharaoh Necho

River Nile

Persian Gulf

Red Sea

■ Nebuchadnezzar's invasions
□ Judean exiles taken to Babylon

So the curtain fell at last on the history of Judah and for about fifty years the majority of the people remained as exiles in Babylon. Then the inevitable happened once more. The mighty nation of Babylon, having conquered the Near East from Assyria in the north to Egypt in the south, reached the zenith of its power, and began to decline. This time it was the turn of the Persians to eclipse the glory of a previous empire, and with them came new hope and life for the Jews and Judah.

As the capital of a powerful empire, Babylon was a splendid city with many impressive buildings. These are remains of the palace of Nebuchadnezzar II.

The teaching of Jeremiah

Anyone who is known as 'a Jeremiah' is normally thought to be mournful and pessimistic. The prophet who lent his name to such a dubious characteristic was certainly full of woe. He seems to have been a highly sensitive person, who could be both affectionately gentle and aggressively outspoken. He was passionately concerned that the people of Judah should worship and serve God wholeheartedly, and he suffered considerably for telling them so. He was laughed at, despised, and continually harassed, and there were at least two attempts on his life (26:8-9; 36:26). As a result of people's indifference to his message, he often became depressed and even suicidal.

His work spanned the lives of five kings (Josiah, Jehoahaz, Jehoiakim, Jehoiachin and Zedekiah) and lasted for about forty years. His message was adapted to the needs of the people at particular times, but certain themes are common throughout his book.

The one true God

To Jeremiah there could be only one God, Yahweh, the God of Israel. He was a God who maintained the physical order he had originally created (31:35-37). He could do anything; 'is anything too hard for me?' he asked (32:26). He gave life to people and also knew what they were thinking (17:7-13). He ruled not only over the fortunes of Judah, but also over all other nations as well.

Their gods, by contrast, being merely 'the work of men's

hands', were unable to match his greatness. Jeremiah names several of them, including Baal, Moloch and the Queen of heaven, which implies that idolatry was fairly widespread in Judah. There were even idols in the temple and child sacrifices were made in the Hinnom Valley outside Jerusalem (32:34-35).

Standards of behaviour

Jeremiah was a stern critic of the accepted behaviour patterns of his time. He condemned injustice, envy, violence, murder and adultery, all of which appear to have been common and tolerated. He contradicted the popular proverb that the effects of disobeying God in one generation would not be felt until the next (31:29) and emphasized individual responsibility for wrongdoing.

Although standards were low, religion was popular, and much of Jeremiah's criticism was reserved for the priests and other religious leaders who condoned or encouraged the contemporary way of life. He foretold the destruction of the temple as a punishment for Judah's apostasy, together with the end of the sacrificial system and priestly organization. Only a radical change of attitude would avert the impending catastrophe of defeat and exile to Babylon, he prophesied. And as that was not forthcoming, he looked further ahead to a day when a genuine renewal of religion would occur.

The new covenant

Jeremiah, more than any other Old Testament prophet, anticipated some of the major teachings of Christianity. This is one of the reasons why his book is so important. In chapter 31 he looks forward to a day when God will make a new covenant with Israel and Judah. It will supercede the old covenant made with Moses on Mount Sinai. Instead of God's law being a written code of instructions, his will and purpose will be engraved in the hearts and minds of his followers. The people will serve God as an act of love, not as a troublesome duty.

Jesus took up this theme at the 'last supper', the meal he shared with his closest followers shortly before he was crucified. 'This is my blood of the new covenant,' he said, as he passed the cup of wine round the group. And the earliest Christian preachers spoke of the risen Christ dwelling in the lives of his followers, creating a new bond of love and obedience between them and God.

Jeremiah's book

The prophet's visions and messages were written down, and the result is the longest book in the Bible. It has some similarities with the Book of Deuteronomy, and some phrases and passages in Jeremiah seem to echo it. If the book found by Josiah's workmen was also Deuteronomy, Jeremiah would certainly have been very familiar with it.

In common with some other prophets and teachers in ancient times, Jeremiah dictated his book to a scribe. This man, Baruch, appears to have been one of the few companions the lonely prophet had (chapter 36).

Questions of life and death

Israel's religious leaders included not only prophets and priests, but also 'wise men' (see Jeremiah 18:18). They were often respected members of the king's court. Their teaching was based on many years' experience and observation of life. They gave advice about how people should live, and grappled with difficult questions such as why innocent people suffer.

The books written by these wise men have been influenced by ideas from other ancient Near Eastern countries. Before the biblical books of Proverbs, Job and Ecclesiastes (which we call 'wisdom literature') were written, wise men in Mesopotamia and Egypt had been writing down their reflections on life.

These, for example, are three proverbs from Mesopotamia:

'Last year I ate garlic, this year my inside burns.'

'He who digs a pit for his neighbour fills it with his own body.'

'As long as a man does not exert himself, he will gain nothing.'

And these are from Egypt:

'Do not talk a lot. Be silent, and you will be happy.'

'Better is bread, when the heart is happy, than riches with sorrow.'

There were longer works too, such as a Babylonian *Dialogue about Human Misery* (about 1000–700 BC), dealing with the same theme as the book of Job. Much earlier is the Egyptian *Instruction of Ptah-Hotep* (about 2450 BC), a collection of advice for aspiring court officials.

The wise men of Israel used what was good from such teaching, but there was always a distinctly Israelite flavour to their wise sayings. Underlying their teaching was the belief that 'the fear of the Lord is the beginning of wisdom' (Proverbs 9:10). Wisdom to them was not just cleverness, but practical insight into the meaning and purpose of life.

King Solomon was thought of as the supreme example of the Israelite wise men. Some of the sayings in the book of Proverbs were made up or collected by him, and other wisdom writings were later attributed to him.

The Book of Proverbs

The proverbs in this book were collected over several hundred years. Most of them give practical and common-sense advice, based on experience of how things work out in life.

Some are simple statements

used to advise young people: 'A wise son makes a glad father, but a foolish son is a sorrow to his mother' (10:1).

Others make comparisons between human life and the world of nature: 'Like clouds and wind without rain is a man who boasts of a gift he does not give' (25:14). Some make their point with humour: 'As a door turns on its hinge, so does a lazy man on his bed' (26:14).

Other proverbs warn of the danger of drinking too much alcohol (20:1), of trying to get rich quickly (28:20), and of being deceived by the charms of an immoral woman (5:3). Such things may look attractive, but they lead to sin and despair.

The wise man has observed life keenly:

'Three things are too
   wonderful for me;
four I do not understand:
the way of an eagle in the sky,
the way of a serpent on a rock,

the way of a ship on the high
  seas,
and the way of a man with a
  maiden' (30:18-19).
And he knows the value of the
wisdom which God gives:
  'Trust in the Lord with all your
    heart,
  and do not rely on your own
    insight.
  In all your ways acknowledge
    him,
  and he will make straight your
    paths.
  Be not wise in your own eyes;
  fear the Lord, and turn away
    from evil.
  It will be healing to your flesh
  and refreshment to your
    bones' (3:5-8).

The Book of Job

Other writers saw that life is not
always as straightforward as
Proverbs seems to suggest. One
such person wrote the story of
Job, a man whose faith in God
was tested by extreme suffering.

The story opens with a picture
of Job as a religious, happy and
wealthy man. But a question is
raised. Does Job trust and
worship God only because he
thinks that as a result he will get
the blessings of health, riches
and a happy family? So God
allows Job to suffer the loss of all
his wealth, and even his
children, to test whether his love
for God is genuine.

In the book's long central
section Job discusses with his
friends, who represent the pious
orthodoxy of the day, why such
suffering has come upon him.
They suggest that it must be a
punishment for his sins. But Job
cannot think of anything he has
done to deserve such pain and
sorrow. He finds his sufferings a
great puzzle.

Finally God himself speaks out
of a whirlwind. Does Job
imagine, God asks, that he can
understand everything in the
world? Was Job present when
the world was made? There are
some questions Job cannot
answer, and the cause of
suffering is one of them. The

really important thing – in the
face of both suffering and
blessing – is to recognize the
greatness of God and to trust him.

Job realizes that he has not
been trusting God; he has been
demanding answers from God
which it is not right for him to
receive. He turns again to God in
trust, and discovers a deeper
relationship with God than he
knew before:
  'I had heard of you by the
    hearing of the ear,
  but now my eye sees you;
  therefore I despise myself,
  and repent in dust and
    ashes' (42:5-6).
And in the end God restored Job
to health, happiness, and even
greater riches than he had
before.

The book of Job does not give
a solution to the problem of
suffering and reveals the
inadequacy of glib answers. It is
really a book about man's
relationship to God. If a person is
willing to trust God, even when
things happen to him which he
cannot understand, he will know
God in a deep and real way.

Some of the deep questions
which Job asks receive a fuller
answer in the New Testament.
For example, 'How can a man be
just before God?' (9:2) is the
theme of Paul's explanation of
Jesus' death in Romans 5. 'If a
man dies, shall he live again?'
(14:14) is answered, again by
Paul, in a discussion of the
resurrection of Jesus in
1 Corinthians 15. And the cry 'O
that I knew where I might find
him!' (23:3) is put in a new
perspective by the New
Testament insistence that God
revealed himself as a man in
Jesus Christ.

The Book of Ecclesiastes

The author of this book
('Ecclesiastes' means 'the
preacher'), like the authors of
Proverbs, has studied human life
closely. He tells us what he has
observed, and concludes – like
Job – that it is not as easy to find
meaning in life as Proverbs

seems to suggest.

He says in chapter 2 that he has
looked in many directions to find
the meaning of life. He has tried
pleasure, entertainment,
enjoyment of food and drink,
hard work in achieving
greatness, and making and
spending money. Yet all these,
he concludes, are 'vanity, and a
striving after wind' (2:17). They
are empty, their value vanishes
like steam from hot water. Even
the pursuit of wisdom cannot
save a person from dying and
being forgotten as quickly as a
fool.

The preacher knows that God
has made the world, and man
can do little to change it:
'Consider the work of God; who
can make straight what he has
made crooked?' (7:13). It seems
impossible to understand God's
purposes; even though 'for
everything there is a season, and
a time for every matter under
heaven' (3:1), we 'cannot find out
what God has done from the
beginning to the end' (3:11).
Death in particular mocks all
man's attempts to enjoy life and
to find meaning in it. People die
just as animals do; 'all go to one
place' (3:20).

Yet the preacher does not
completely despair of life. Even
though he cannot understand
God's purposes, he still believes
that God *has* a purpose. He can
take courage from that, even
though his observations of life
have led him to doubt much of
what he has been taught about
religion. His task is not to try and
discover God's purpose in
everything but to use wisely the
opportunities that are presented
to him each day.

The book appeals widely to
people today, especially those
deeply aware of the apparent
futility of life and who ask the
important questions about the
purpose of human life. The
book's despair, that death brings
an end to life and hope, is met by
the New Testament's faith in a life
with Christ beyond death.

THE END OF AN ERA

The Old Testament narrative ends about 500 years before the birth of John the Baptist and the start of the New Testament story. It records few events after the Jews returned to Jerusalem from exile in Babylon during the sixth and fifth centuries BC. Yet those 500 years before Christ saw the development of the Jewish religion as Jesus knew it. During this time successive military conquests in Palestine radically affected Jewish life and customs. Just as New Testament teaching needs to be interpreted in the light of the Jewish beliefs and principles, so the world of the New Testament, in the first century AD, can be fully understood only in the light of events which took place in the preceding centuries.

The end of the exile

The Jews' forced exile in Babylon lasted for about fifty years. They came to believe that God was punishing them severely for their past sins. But at last the opportunity came for them to return home.

After the death of King Nebuchadnezzar, the end of the Babylonian Empire came unexpectedly quickly. To the east of Babylonia was the kingdom of Persia, ruled by Cyrus. In 550 BC, he conquered Media to the north; in 546 he gained control of the rich kingdom of Lydia (in present-day Turkey).

Eventually he captured Babylon itself by diverting the course of the River Euphrates. His army entered the city along the dried-up river bed. Babylon was already demoralized and discontented with its own leaders, and there was little resistance to the invader.

Cyrus now controlled an empire stretching 3,000 miles/5,000km from Lydia in the west to India in the east. He

The Persian Empire

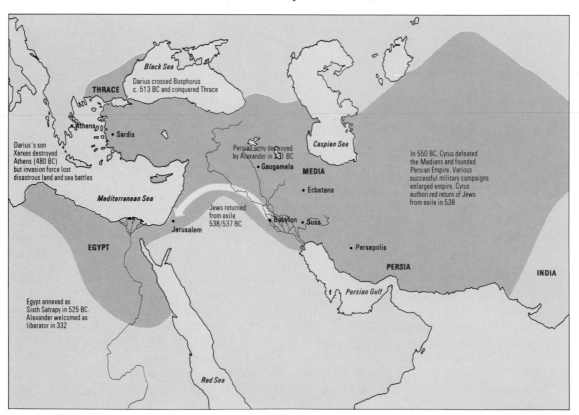

Black Sea

Darius crossed Bosphorus
c. 513 BC and conquered Thrace

THRACE

Athens

Sardis

Darius's son Xerxes destroyed Athens (480 BC) but invasion force lost disastrous land and sea battles

Caspian Sea

Persian army destroyed by Alexander in 331 BC

Gaugamela

MEDIA

Ecbatana

In 550 BC, Cyrus defeated the Medians and founded Persian Empire. Various successful military campaigns enlarged empire. Cyrus authorized return of Jews from exile in 538

Mediterranean Sea

Jews returned from exile 538/537 BC

Babylon

Susa

Jerusalem

EGYPT

Persepolis

Egypt annexed as Sixth Satrapy in 525 BC. Alexander welcomed as liberator in 332

PERSIA

INDIA

Persian Gulf

Red Sea

organized his empire by dividing it into twenty provinces or 'satrapies', each with its own governor ('satrap'). Judah was in the satrapy of 'Transpotamia' ('across the river', i.e. the Euphrates).

Rebuilding in Judah

Cyrus' policy was to send all exiles back to their own countries. So after fifty years in exile in Babylon, the Jews could go home. But they did not all rush to pack their bags and set off to Judah. Most of them had been born in Babylon. They saw it as their home. Many of them had thriving businesses there, and had no wish to leave.

Judah itself was in a bad state. The few peasants who had been left behind during the exile had tried to cultivate the land. But enemies of the Jews, including Moabites and Edomites, kept raiding the land. And Jerusalem remained in ruins.

However, some Jews did go back to Judah, led by Shesh-bezzar (son of King Jehoiachin), Zerubbabel (Jehoiachin's grandson) and Joshua the high priest. They took with them the temple treasures which Nebuchadnezzar had removed in

Babylon: city of promise

Babylon was a large and splendid city with many parks and gardens. Nebuchadnezzar II had built many fine, ornate palaces with beautiful decorations and carvings. The 'hanging gardens' on the roof of his personal palace were regarded as one of the seven wonders of the world.

There were many navigable waterways running through the city and connecting it with outlying settlements. The Jews (and other national groups exiled with them) lived mainly in internment camps beside these waterways.

Life in the camps was not hard. The Jews were allowed to build houses for themselves and cultivate the land. Some of them soon became involved in the commerce of the city and became prosperous. This was why many of them refused to return home to Judah when Cyrus gave them the opportunity. Life was too good in Babylon for all but the most dedicated to face the hardships

of the long journey and rebuilding their home. And Babylonian customs seemed more interesting and profitable than their traditional customs.

However, many of the Jews continued to worship God, even in Babylon. Their prophets, Ezekiel, in exile with them in Babylon, and Jeremiah, who sent messages from Jerusalem, encouraged prayer and fasting as did the exiled priests.

Although they could not worship at the temple or offer sacrifices, they kept the traditional feasts and sabbath days, and held house meetings for instruction in the law of God. These practices were the forerunners of the synagogue worship of later generations of Jews.

The illustration is an artist's impression of part of the city of Babylon, based on archaeological excavations.

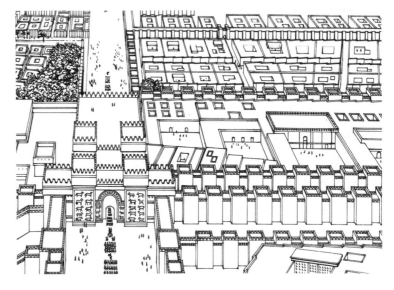

The Persians

The Kingdom of Persia expanded suddenly in the sixth century BC when Cyrus II defeated Media, conquered Assyria, Babylonia, Asia Minor and lands as far east as India. He adopted the best aspects of the laws and religions of conquered nations for the benefit of his empire – the greatest the world had yet known. The Persian Empire's power and wealth can be deduced from the remains of magnificent buildings at ancient capitals like Pasargadae and Persepolis. Columns were decorated with carvings, and richly-patterned textiles adorned the great halls. Skilled goldsmiths fashioned jewellery and other ornaments.

Below: a ninth-century BC Persian axe-head; a capital from Susa, made of grey marble, dating from the fifth or fourth century BC.

A bowman ('immortal') of the Persian royal guard.

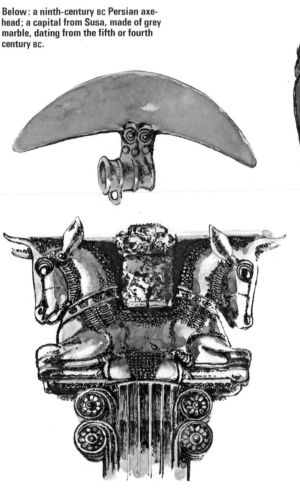

Right: a Persian ostrich-hunt.

Below: this group, based on a palace relief from Persepolis, shows King Darius I of Persia (521–486 BC) seated on an elaborate throne, with a matching footstool, and holding a long sceptre or staff. Behind him stands the Crown Prince, Xerxes, with a servant in the background. Two palace guards are also in attendance, while a nobleman comes forward to speak to the king. The two incense-burners mark the point beyond which visitors must not pass.

587 BC. For some years they lived in Judah, doing nothing to rebuild the temple.

About 537 BC they made a start on the rebuilding, but did not

Haggai 1:1-11

carry on long. Then, in 520 BC the prophet Haggai criticized the people for being too concerned about their own affairs and neglecting to rebuild God's house, the temple. With his encouragement they set to work on restoring the temple, and in 515 BC the work was finished. It was not as splendid as Solomon's original building, but at least they had a temple again, and there was great rejoicing.

The return to Judah was not quite as exciting as people expected. There was much work to be done rebuilding the ruins and providing enough food for the families. Also the

Malachi 1:6–2:17

prophet Malachi said that the people were not sincere in their religion, and the priests were not guiding the people as they should. Rich men were exploiting the poor, and mixed marriages with pagan women were common. To try to encourage the Jews and draw them back to God, Ezra and Nehemiah returned to Judah.

Ezra teaches the law

The Persian emperor was now Artaxerxes I, and he allowed Ezra to travel back from Babylonia to Judah in 458 BC. Ezra was a scholar and an expert in the Jewish law.

During the exile, he and other experts had been writing out

Exodus 20:1-17

the law in its final form. Originally, God's law had been given to Moses on Mount Sinai. But for centuries much of it was passed on verbally and it was revised as new situations arose. Now it was finally written down in great detail, and brought back to Jerusalem by Ezra and his companions.

Nehemiah 8:1-8

Ezra read out the law to a great assembly of the Jews near the temple. It was written in Hebrew, which the ordinary people did not understand, and so interpreters explained it in

The Aramaic language

The main language of Cyrus' Empire was Aramaic, and many of the emperor's official documents were written in it. It was an ancient language, known to Jewish officials as early as the time of Hezekiah. It was very similar to Hebrew. It had the same alphabet because Hebrew actually took over Aramaic script, but different rules of grammar. As Jews returned from Babylon

to Palestine, they brought the language with them.

Gradually the ordinary people forgot how to speak the ancient Hebrew in which most of their scriptures were written. (Parts of the books of Ezra and Daniel were originally in Aramaic, but the rest of the Old Testament was written in Hebrew.) They could not understand the Old Testament unless they took the trouble to learn Hebrew, or had it explained to them by a scholar. An instance of this is

recorded in Nehemiah 8:8.

By the time of Jesus Aramaic was still the Jews' everyday language and the scriptures had been translated into it. A few of Jesus' sayings in Aramaic are quoted in Mark's Gospel. (For example, when Jesus healed a little girl who had died, Mark 5:41.) It was not until 1948, when the modern state of Israel was set up, that Hebrew once again became the ordinary language of Jews in Palestine.

Aramaic as Ezra went along. When they heard the law, the people saw that many things in their lives were not according to God's will, and they began to put them right. The laws which they heard at that assembly are those now included in the first five books of the Old Testament (Genesis to Deuteronomy).

To rebuild the walls of Jerusalem, Nehemiah divided his labour force: half worked on the wall while the rest formed an armed guard. At the Western ('Wailing') Wall in Jerusalem, a modern Israeli soldier has a phylactery, containing passages of the Jewish law, wound onto his arm.

Nehemiah rebuilds the walls

Nehemiah was cup-bearer to the Emperor Artaxerxes, and lived at Susa, one of the Persian royal capitals. He served the emperor's wine, but he also had to taste it first to make sure it was not poisoned. Cup-bearers were often trusted advisers and friends of the rulers they served.

When Nehemiah's brother Hanani arrived from Judah to report that the walls of Jerusalem were broken down, and enemies were continually attacking the city, Nehemiah was upset. He decided to ask the emperor's permission to rebuild the walls himself. Artaxerxes approved of his plan, and actually made him governor of Judah.

Nehemiah 2:11-18

Nehemiah arrived in Jerusalem about 445 BC. First he made a secret inspection of the walls by night, to decide how the work should be done. Then he organized the whole population of the city to work on the rebuilding.

Nehemiah 4:1-23

The work was not easy. Governors of the nearby districts of Samaria, Ammon and Arabia did all they could to hinder the building. They knew that if Judah became strong again their own safety might be threatened. But Nehemiah refused to be put off. He made half his men stand guard while the other half built the walls.

In fifty-two days they had patched up the worst gaps in the walls, though the complete work of rebuilding took over two years. Now Jerusalem was secure again.

Jerusalem

Jerusalem has been the stage on which some of history's most dramatic events have taken place. It is still a focus of interest in the world today. It has probably been besieged, destroyed and rebuilt more often than any other famous city. A succession of conquerors – including Egyptians, Assyrians, Babylonians, and Romans – all saw the capture of Jerusalem as crucial to their overall strategy of empire-building in the Near East. It was the scene for much of the activity described in the Bible, and is a 'holy city' for three faiths – Judaism, Islam and Christianity.

There may have been a settlement on the site of present-day Jerusalem as long ago as around 2900 BC. The city is first mentioned in written records (inscriptions on Egyptian bowls) about 1,000 years later in the nineteenth century BC, as a city of the Canaanites. The site was probably chosen because its hilltop location and constant water supply from the Gihon Spring meant

Above: the walls of Jerusalem from the time of the Jebusites, King Hezekiah (about 715 BC) and Suleiman the Magnificent (AD 1536), with some modern retaining walls.

that it could be easily fortified and defended. However, there are no special physical or economic advantages which explain why Jerusalem should ever have become more than an anonymous village in the Judean hills.

When the Israelites entered Canaan in the middle of the thirteenth century BC, Jerusalem (then called Jebus) was occupied by a local tribe, the Jebusites. They were not ousted for some 250 years, until King David unified the settled tribes of Israel. He conquered the strategic site of Jerusalem and made it his capital city.

David set about making Jerusalem the political, military and religious centre of the country. His son Solomon carried this further

with an extensive building programme in the capital. The building of the temple (on the highest spot of the hilltop site) took seven years of Solomon's reign.

When the kingdom was divided in about 930 BC, Jerusalem was capital only of the two southern tribes, Judah and Benjamin. Later kings strengthened the city's fortifications and withstood attacks from would-be invaders. King Hezekiah (715–687 BC), under threat of an Assyrian siege, sealed off the Gihon Spring from the outside to deny the enemy a water supply and ensure his own. He then had a 600-yard/ 550-metre tunnel dug to carry water inside the city walls to the Pool of Siloam, which acted as a reservoir.

In 587 BC, Jerusalem fell to the Babylonians who destroyed and burnt the city and tore down the walls. Jewish survivors were exiled to Babylon. Their dream of returning to Jerusalem was fulfilled in 539 BC when the Persians conquered Babylon and allowed the Jews to go back. They rebuilt a more modest version of Solomon's

Jerusalem at the time of the kings

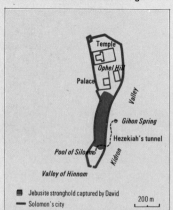

Temple
Ophel Hill
Palace
Valley
Gihon Spring
Hezekiah's tunnel
Pool of Siloam
Kidron
Valley of Hinnom

▪ Jebusite stronghold captured by David
— Solomon's city
200 m

Jerusalem at the time of Nehemiah

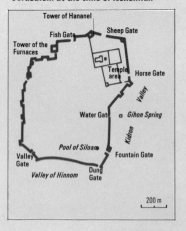

Tower of Hananel
Fish Gate
Sheep Gate
Tower of the Furnaces
Temple area
Horse Gate
Valley
Water Gate
Gihon Spring
Pool of Siloam
Kidron
Valley Gate
Fountain Gate
Valley of Hinnom
Dung Gate
200 m

grand temple. The city walls remained in ruins until Nehemiah restored them in the middle of the fifth century BC.

Jerusalem, with Judea, was ruled by the Persians from 537–332 BC, but little is known about this period. When the city's name reappeared in history, Alexander the Great was claiming an empire for Greece, and Jerusalem automatically became part of his realm when he succeeded the Persian (Achaemenid) kings.

With Alexander's death, Jerusalem came under the control of the Egyptian king Ptolemy and the Jews enjoyed considerable freedom for self-government. The third century BC was a relatively stable period and Jerusalem developed and prospered.

But in 175 BC Antiochus IV, Epiphanes, succeeded to the throne of Syria and tried to advance the worship of Greek gods. He set up a pagan statue in the Jerusalem temple. Failure to observe the pagan customs was punished by death, and from 167–141 BC the Jews fought back in the Maccabaean Wars of Liberation. The Temple Mount in Jerusalem was retaken in 164 BC and the temple rededicated, allowing the Jews to resume their sacrifices.

About eighty years of political independence from foreigners came to an end in 63 BC when the Roman general Pompey entered the city and brought Judea under Roman control. But rather than ruling the area directly, the Roman Senate put Herod the Great on the throne of Judea in 37 BC. Although hated by the Jews, he was responsible for many splendid buildings being constructed in Jerusalem, including a new temple, an imposing fortress (Fort Antonia) and a royal palace.

Many events in Jesus' life took place in Jerusalem, most notably his crucifixion and resurrection; it was from Jerusalem that his disciples went out to other areas to proclaim the Christian faith.

Looking at the splendour of Herod's temple in Jerusalem one day, Jesus prophesied its destruction (Matthew 24:1-2). This prophecy was amply fulfilled in AD 70 when, after about four years of guerrilla-type warfare by Jewish revolutionary groups throughout Judea, the Romans, led by Titus, captured Jerusalem after 139 days of struggle. They burned the temple and left the city in ruins. Tens of thousands of prisoners were taken, and were either sold as slaves or forced to fight as gladiators. Exile was once again the normal condition for most Jews; but Jerusalem, though destroyed, remained their spiritual home and object of their devotion.

The war of freedom led by Simon Bar Kochba in AD 132–5 briefly made Jerusalem the Jewish capital once again, but in 135 the Emperor Hadrian totally destroyed it, then rebuilt it and called it Aelia Capitolina. And once again the city passed from hand to hand. The Persians captured it in AD 614, the Moslems in 638, the Crusaders in 1099, the Turks in 1517. The British entered it during the First World War, and after the Second World War, in 1948, the State of Israel was proclaimed. Jerusalem was declared the capital in the following year.

Religious sites of Moslems and Christians have been maintained and fresh archaeological work, notably on the ancient city walls, has been undertaken. But apart from the old city itself, Jerusalem today is typical of many modern cities, with busy streets, stores and offices.

Jerusalem at the time of Christ

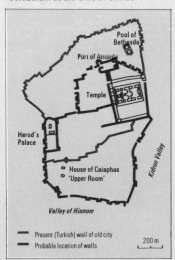

Pool of Bethesda

Fort of Antonia

Temple

Herod's Palace

House of Caiaphas
'Upper Room'

Kidron Valley

Valley of Hinnom

— Present (Turkish) wall of old city
— Probable location of walls

200 m

Right: a typical street in the old city of Jerusalem.

The Samaritans

The story of the good Samaritan is probably the most well-known of the many parables that Jesus told. A passing Samaritan helped the Jewish victim of a highway robbery, while fellow Jews – even religious leaders – did not want to risk getting involved.

It was a pointed lesson; the Samaritans were regarded as scum – 'untouchables' – by the Jews. This hatred and disdain arose largely because the Jews did not consider the Samaritans to be of pure Hebrew blood. They also felt that the Samaritans had contaminated the worship of God with that of idols.

King Omri (885–874 BC) of Israel bought a hilltop site about 6 miles/10km north-west of Shechem. On it he built his capital, which he called Samaria, possibly meaning the 'watch-

Samaritans still celebrate the Passover on Mt Gerizim and are the only group in Israel who continue to sacrifice animals.

post'. The site was well chosen for defence and Samaria continued to be the capital of the ten northern tribes until the collapse of the kingdom of Israel and the capture of the city by the Assyrians in 722 BC.

Samaria became notorious for its idol-worship. King Ahab, the son of Omri, built a temple and an altar to the Canaanite god, Baal, there. Along with pagan religious practices came moral corruption and the prophets were constantly warning the people of Samaria about God's judgement.

It eventually came. The Assyrians captured the city in 722 BC and organized a mass deportation of the Jews the following year. The exiles were sent to Syria, Assyria and Babylonia, and the land was re-populated with colonists from other disturbed parts of the Assyrian Empire.

The Samaritans were the descendants of the Israelites who remained in the northern

kingdom and intermarried with this newly-imported alien population. The Jews of the southern kingdom spurned social and religious association with them and the rift widened as time went on. When Nehemiah was supervising the rebuilding of the walls of Jerusalem (about 440 BC), leading Samaritans were among those who opposed and ridiculed the work.

The date of the building of the Samaritan temple on Mount Gerizim, overlooking Shechem, is unknown, but this act set the seal on the Jewish rejection of this 'heretical sect'. The final breach between Jews and Samaritans had probably occurred by about 200 BC. At the time of the Maccabaean Revolt, the Samaritans compromised to please Antiochus IV, called 'Epiphanes', and dedicated their temple to the Greek god Zeus. The Jewish king Hyrcanus destroyed the Samaritan temple in 128 BC; however, worship continued on the summit of Mount Gerizim where the temple had stood.

A small community of Samaritans still lives in Israel today, at Nablus (formerly Shechem). They celebrate the Passover by making a pilgrimage to Mount Gerizim and setting up tents, one for each family. Lambs are sacrificed at sunset and later roasted according to the high priest's instructions. Meat and ritual food is portioned out and the Samaritans stay awake until dawn reciting prayers.

Their religious authority is the Samaritan Pentateuch – the Five Books of Moses (Genesis to Deuteronomy). The Samaritan creed has six articles: belief in one God, in Moses the prophet, in the law, in Mount Gerizim as the place appointed by God for sacrifice, in a day of judgement and recompense and in the return of Moses as a 'restorer' (similar to the Jewish hope of a coming messiah).

The development of Jewish religion

During the time of the Maccabaean Wars the two main Jewish parties which feature prominently in the New Testament began to emerge.

Pharisees

The Pharisees came from those who had supported the Maccabaean Revolt because they loved the Jewish law. They were glad when the Maccabees won religious freedom, because the Jews could now obey their law without fear of persecution. But when the Jewish kings became more interested in military conquest than in religious observance, they lost their support.

The Pharisees tried to live in obedience to all the details of

A Jewish rabbi and his son. The father wears the round, fur-bordered hat and both have the side curls characteristic of strict orthodox Jews.

Jewish festivals

The Jews, like most people, loved celebrations. Every year they had three great 'pilgrimage festivals', for which people travelled to Jerusalem from all over Palestine. Travelling in groups, they would sing psalms such as those collected in Psalms 120–134. Each of these psalms is called 'a song of ascents', because it was used by people ascending (going up) to Jerusalem, the city in the hills of Judea. This psalm expresses their joy at being present for the festival:

> I was glad when they said to
>   me,
> 'Let us go to the house of the
>   Lord!'
> Our feet have been standing
>   within your gates, O
>   Jerusalem!
>   (Psalm 122:1-2)

The way in which festivals were celebrated developed over the centuries. During the time of the kings of Judah (about 900–600 BC) the festival calendar included the following major events.

The Feast of Passover and Unleavened Bread

Exodus 12; Leviticus 23:5-8; Numbers 28:16-25

This festival occurred every spring (March-April). Like other festivals, it was both a celebration and a commemoration of God's acts in Israel's history. The Jews gave thanks for the beginning of the barley harvest, and for God's deliverance of their ancestors from slavery in Egypt.

On the evening of the full moon, each family had a year-old lamb sacrificed at the temple in Jerusalem. They then took it home – or to their lodgings, if they were pilgrims from other parts of Palestine. There they ate it, with bitter herbs and unleavened bread (bread made without yeast), at the Passover meal.

Next day the Feast of Unleavened Bread began. Any old, leavened bread (bread with yeast in it) which remained in the house was destroyed. For seven days they ate only unleavened bread, using the grain from the new harvest. The unleavened bread also reminded them of the haste in which the Israelites had eaten on the first Passover night, before their escape from Egypt.

The Feast of Weeks

Exodus 34:22; Leviticus 23:15-21

This took place in May-June, seven weeks after Passover: hence its name. Later it was also called Pentecost. (*Pentecoste* is Greek for 'fiftieth' – the fiftieth day after Passover.) But it was also called simply Harvest (Exodus 23:16), because it marked the end of the wheat harvest. Two loaves were made of new wheat-flour and baked with yeast, then offered to God in the temple.

It was only after the Old Testament period that the Jews connected this festival with God's action in their history. Not long before the time of Jesus, they began to include in the Feast of Weeks a celebration of the covenant God made with Moses at Mount Sinai.

The Feast of Tabernacles

Leviticus 23:33-43; Numbers 29:12-38; Deuteronomy 16:13-15

In Old Testament times the most important festival was that of 'In-gathering' (Exodus 23:16, 34:22) or 'Tabernacles' (Leviticus 23:34, Deuteronomy 16:13). It celebrated the completion of the fruit harvest in September-October. It was an occasion for dancing in the vineyards, and for great rejoicing. A later proverb said: 'The man who has never seen the joy of the night of this feast has never seen real joy in all his life.'

For seven days and nights the pilgrims stayed in Jerusalem in makeshift huts or tents (which is the meaning of the old word 'tabernacle'). Even the

The Passover was one of the most important Jewish festivals and orthodox Jews, like the family in the picture, still celebrate it today. It is a reminder of the way in which God rescued the Israelites from their slavery in Egypt.

permanent inhabitants of the city erected temporary huts outside their normal homes. These huts reminded them of the temporary shelters built of branches in the vineyards and orchards while the grapes and fruit were being gathered in. But the huts reminded them too that the Israelites had lived in tents in the desert when Moses led them out of Egypt to Canaan.

On each day of the festival bulls, rams, lambs and goats were sacrificed in the temple, and portions of wheat-flour and wine were offered to God. The final, eighth day of the festival was marked by a grand assembly at the temple, before the pilgrims departed to their homes.

use in Esther 3:7 of *pur*, an Assyrian word meaning 'lot'.) But thanks to the bravery of Esther – a Jewish girl whom the Persian king had married – and her cousin Mordecai, the plot was discovered. Haman was hanged on the gallows he had prepared for Mordecai, and the Jews were able to destroy the men sent to kill them.

This story may have its historical origin in events during the fifth or fourth century BC. In any case, the Feast of Purim which celebrated this remarkable deliverance of the Jews arose much later than the other festivals of the Old Testament. And it was more of a carnival than a solemn religious festival. A day of fasting was followed by two days of rejoicing during February-March. The book of Esther was read in the synagogue, and the congregation shouted and booed every time Haman was mentioned. People gave presents to each other, and enjoyed banquets and all kinds of entertainment.

Apart from the three great pilgrim festivals, other feasts also developed during the Old Testament period. These, like the three great feasts, are still celebrated by Jews today.

The Day of Atonement (Yom Kippur)
Leviticus 16
This festival occurs in September-October, just before the Feast of Tabernacles. It was a day of solemn fasting and repentance, when the Jews asked God's forgiveness for the sins of the last year. The high priest sacrificed a bull for his own sins and for those of the other priests, and a goat for the rest of the people. He entered behind the curtain which shut off the most sacred place in the temple (the 'holy of holies'). There he sprinkled the blood of the bull and the goat on the 'mercy-seat', where God's presence was believed to rest.

This was the only day of the year when anyone was allowed to enter the holy of holies.

Afterwards, another goat was brought to the high priest. He placed his hands on its head, as if to transfer to it all the sins of the people. The goat was then led off into the desert, carrying with it the sins of the Israelites. In this vivid way they acted out their belief that God forgives those who sincerely confess their sins to him.

The Feast of Purim
Esther 9:20-32
The book of Esther in the Old Testament tells how the Jews of Susa in Persia got their revenge on enemies who had planned to kill them. Haman, the chief minister to the Persian king, wanted to murder all the Jews in Persia. Being a superstitious man, he cast lots to discover when he should do it. (The name, 'Feast of Purim', comes from the

The Feast of Hanukkah
1 Maccabees 4:36-59; John 10:22
This festival – often called in English the Festival of Dedication – was introduced in 164 BC, when the temple in Jerusalem was reconsecrated. This followed the victory by Judas Maccabaeus over the Syrian oppressor Antiochus Epiphanes, who had desecrated the temple by offering pigs in sacrifice to the Greek god Zeus.

It was a joyful feast, lasting eight days in December. There were sacrifices in the temple, and palm-branches were carried in procession. Hymns – especially Psalms 113-118 – were sung. Another prominent feature was the use of lights. Lamps were lit in front of each house, the number being increased by one each day until the last day of the feast. Even today, it is one of the most popular and splendid Jewish festivals.

the Old Testament law. They also added to it new oral teachings, which were not written down, but were intended to apply the old written law to every situation in life. For instance, they defined what could and could not be counted as work on the sabbath. Jesus was later to accuse them of being so over-concerned with detail that they neglected the 'weightier matters of the law' – issues of justice and fairness, for instance.

Sadducees

The Sadducees mainly belonged to the old priestly families. They were not as numerous as the Pharisees, but they were wealthy and important. Many of them were more interested in gaining political power than in practising religion.

    The Sadducees accepted the written law of the first five books of the Old Testament, but rejected the Pharisees' unwritten laws. They also rejected the Pharisees' belief in angels, and in resurrection after death. Paul later exploited *Acts 23* this difference when on trial before the Jewish leaders in Jerusalem. Believing in the resurrection of Jesus, he said to his accusers: 'I am a Pharisee, a son of Pharisees; with respect to the hope and the resurrection of the dead I am on trial.' The meeting broke up in confusion.

Essenes

A third group was the Essenes. They are not in fact mentioned in the New Testament, but they have become well-known since the discovery of the Dead Sea Scrolls. These scrolls belonged to an Essene community who lived as monks at Qumran near the Dead Sea. Some of the scrolls are books of the Old Testament, some are Jewish writings which were not included in the Old Testament, and others are books which members of the Qumran community wrote themselves. They hid the scrolls in caves near their monastery when the Romans invaded Judea in AD 66. The dry climate preserved them in the caves until they were discovered there in 1947.

    The Qumran community was started soon after the Maccabaean Wars by devout Jews who felt that religious life in Jerusalem was becoming corrupt. They aimed, by strict observance of the Jewish law, to prepare for the coming of God's messiah. They felt that by living in their monastery in the *Isaiah 40:3* desert at Qumran they were obeying the word of Isaiah: 'In the wilderness prepare the way of the Lord, make straight in the desert a highway for our God.'

The hope for a messiah

The hope that God would one day send great blessings on his people is mentioned several times in the Old Testament. Wickedness would be destroyed, and God's people would dwell in safety and prosperity. Isaiah and some other prophets *Isaiah 9:1-7; 11:1-10* declared that God would send a king, descended from King David, to lead his people into this new period of blessing.

    Later, this coming king was often referred to as 'the

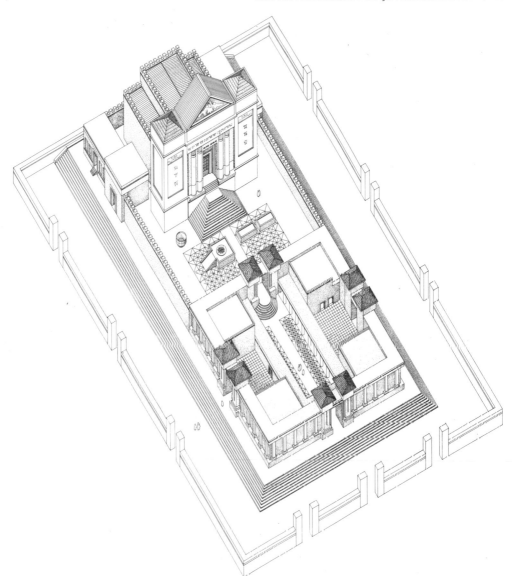

Herod the Great built a temple in Jerusalem largely to win the Jews' favour and impress the Romans. It was far larger and more luxurious than Solomon's temple, and was covered in gold. Non-Jews and traders were not allowed beyond the main wall. Women could go only so far as the round steps in the centre. The priests offered sacrifices on the altars in front of the main temple building. Inside, it was divided into the same two rooms as the tabernacle: the holy place, where incense was offered, and the holy of holies where the high priest went once a year.

messiah', which means 'the anointed one'. (Among the Jews, anyone who was given a special job to do for God, such as a king or a priest, was anointed with oil as a way of appointing him to his task.)

After the Maccabaean Wars, there was increasing hope among the Jews that God would send the messiah soon. The Pharisees hoped for a warrior-messiah who would lead the Jews to victory over their enemies. The Essenes at Qumran believed they were specially chosen by God to prepare the way for the messiah's coming.

When Jesus appeared in Galilee, claiming in word and deed to be that person, he was a rather different kind of messiah from the one most people were expecting . . .

How the Old Testament was compiled

The Bible is a collection of sixty-six books, divided into two main sections: the Old Testament (thirty-nine books) and the New Testament (twenty-seven books). It was written over a period of more than 1,000 years by some forty different authors. But how did the various books come to be written and how were they brought together into the one book we now call the Bible?

The Old Testament contains the holy scriptures of the Jews and their religion, Judaism. The important discovery in 1947 of

A Tunisian rabbi shows his synagogue's scroll of the Torah, or law of God.

the Dead Sea Scrolls in caves at Qumran unearthed the earliest known Hebrew manuscripts of the Old Testament. Copies of all the Old Testament books except Esther were found in complete or fragmentary form. Most of these scrolls date from the first century BC, 1,000 years earlier than the ninth-century AD copies of the first five books of the Bible (the 'Pentateuch') which had previously been the oldest known manuscripts.

Scholars found that the Dead Sea Scrolls had essentially the same text as the ninth-century manuscripts and thus provided evidence of the careful copying done by Jewish scribes. The Jews had obviously preserved their scriptures accurately over many centuries, and this increases confidence in the reliability of the text. Problems still exist, of course; sometimes it is impossible to discover exactly what the original Hebrew words meant and an editor or translator has to be guided by what is most likely.

The Jews arranged their sacred books into three groups: the Law, the Prophets and the Writings. 'The Law' consisted of the Pentateuch, the five books from Genesis to Deuteronomy. The Jews attached great importance to this section because it contained the laws given by God to Moses and also the record of Israel's early history.

'The Prophets' divided into two groups, the 'former' and 'latter' prophets. This section contained the messages of men like Isaiah, Jeremiah and Ezekiel as well as the historical books of Joshua, Judges, Samuel and Kings. 'The Writings' included some later books of history (for instance, Ezra, Nehemiah, Chronicles), the Psalms, the apocalyptic book of Daniel and the Wisdom books of Job, Proverbs, and Ecclesiastes.

We cannot know for certain how the Old Testament books were collected into their present order. It is possible that the scribe Ezra – whose story is in the biblical book Ezra – or other people during his lifetime (the fifth century BC) were engaged in arranging and collecting these sacred books together. This is a strongly-held Jewish tradition. But collections of parts of the Pentateuch, some of the messages of the prophets and some of the psalms and proverbs are known to have existed much earlier than this.

The text of the Old Testament has also been passed down in other translations, some of which help to confirm the accuracy of the Hebrew text. One of the most important of these is the Greek translation, which was probably begun about 250 BC for Jews living in Egypt. Tradition says that seventy translators worked on this version – hence its name 'Septuagint', from a Latin word meaning 'seventy'.

By the time of Jesus, the Hebrew scriptures recognized as authoritative consisted of the thirty-nine books we now know as the Old Testament. They are repeatedly quoted in the New Testament and referred to as 'the scriptures'. It is likely that Jesus and his followers were familiar with the Old Testament as we know it.

The Jews had some additional sacred writings called the *Apocrypha*. These are included in the Greek version of the Old Testament but were never accepted or recognized in the same way as the other Old Testament books and therefore not included in the Hebrew version. Some modern translations of the Bible include the Apocryphal books.

In Jesus' time, the oral law, an interpretation of the written scriptures and an elaboration of some of the principles contained in them, was widely accepted as binding on the Jews. It caused several bitter clashes between the Pharisees and Jesus, who accused them of changing the meaning of the scriptures.

An Outline of The Old Testament Story
In approximate order of main events

APPROX DATES OF MAIN EVENTS (BC) to which books refer (not the date of composition)	BIBLE BOOK	MAIN CHARACTERS	MAIN EVENTS/SUBJECTS	MAIN TEACHING/ RELEVANCE
	GENESIS 1–11	Adam, Noah	Creation of world; people disobey God; the flood; confusion of languages	God is a creator; human sin separates man from God
2000	12–25	Abraham	Abraham travels from Babylon to Palestine	God can be trusted
1900–1700	26–36	Isaac, Jacob	Travels and feuds of the 'patriarchs'	Human stories about men of God
1750–1650	36–50	Joseph	Joseph rejected by his brothers, rises to power in Egypt; famine in many countries	God's purposes in adverse circumstances
1280	EXODUS 1–15	Pharaoh Ramesses II, Moses, Aaron	The plagues in Egypt; the Hebrews escape from slavery	An example of God's power
	16–40	Moses, Aaron	Journey from Red Sea to Mt Sinai; Ten Commandments given; tabernacle built	God's law for all mankind; examples of human disobedience
	LEVITICUS		Religious, dietary and social laws for the Jews; religious festivals outlined	Pictures of how sin can be dealt with; religion to be both serious and joyful
1280–1240	NUMBERS	Moses	Journey from Sinai to Canaan; Korah's revolt	How God leads his people; man's rebellion and God's judgement
	DEUTERONOMY		Boundaries of the promised land; more laws relating to life in Canaan	Challenge to wholehearted faith
1240	JOSHUA	Joshua, Rahab, Achan	Entry into Canaan, capture of key cities; division of the land	Stories of courage – and selfishness
1220–1075	JUDGES	Eli, Samson, Deborah, Gideon	Recurring cycle of disobedience, then attack by enemies, then repentance, as Israel settles into the land	God's righteousness and judgement; examples of dedicated lives
1100–1000	RUTH	Naomi, Ruth, Boaz	Illustration of life in time of the judges	Example of love and devotion to God's people; non-Jews have a place in God's purposes
1075–1035	1 SAMUEL 1–10	Samuel	Israel at war with Philistines; birth of Samuel; demand for a king	Israel succumbs to the desire to be like all the other nations
1050–1010	11–31	Saul and David	Feud between Saul and David; battles with Philistines	God's dealings with an arrogant king and a humble shepherd boy
1010–970	2 SAMUEL	David, Joab, Absalom	Reign of King David; Philistines defeated; Absalom's rebellion	Candid account of the successes and mistakes of a man who tried to follow God
1010–970	1 CHRONICLES	David	David's wars; preparation for the temple; lists of Israelite families	Example of leadership and faith; unfolding of God's purpose for Israel
970–930	1 KINGS 2 CHRONICLES 1–9	Solomon	Solomon's reign, wisdom; building and dedication of temple	Example of a godly leader, and how his folly led to natural disaster

An Outline of The Old Testament Story (continued)
In approximate order of main events

APPROX DATES OF MAIN EVENTS (BC) to which books refer (not the date of composition)	BIBLE BOOK	MAIN CHARACTERS	MAIN EVENTS/SUBJECTS	MAIN TEACHING/ RELEVANCE
930–609	2 KINGS 2 CHRONICLES 10–36	Elijah, Elisha, and a succession of kings and prophets	Israel divided into two kingdoms – north (Israel) and south (Judah); evil kings lead nation to defeat; some good ones bring reforms	God's demands of obedience; examples of faith and prophetic leadership
760	AMOS	Amos; (Jeroboam II of Israel)	Message of judgement against Israel for disobedience, and other nations for cruelty	The necessity for social justice based on Israel's covenant with God
760	JONAH	(Jeroboam II of Israel)	Message of judgement on Nineveh and Jonah's reluctance to deliver it	A challenge to obedience; God's sovereignty and human responsibility; God's concern for non-Jews
740–700	ISAIAH	(Uzziah, Jotham, Ahaz, and Hezekiah, kings of Judah)	Prophecies concerning Judah besieged by the Assyrians; a call to faith and trust in an almighty God	Lofty view of God's power, holiness and love; the need to trust God; prophecies of the exile
750–720	HOSEA	(prophecy to Israel)	Picture of a decadent society and of God's love for them still, shown through Hosea's marriage	Vivid and dramatic reminder of God's love
720	MICAH	(Mainly in reign of Hezekiah, of Judah)	Prophecy of exile as punishment for disobeying God	The need to turn away from wrongdoing
626–587	JEREMIAH	Jeremiah; kings Josiah, Jehoakim and Zedekiah of Judah	Babylonian invasion and exile of Judah; futile attempt at a treaty with Egypt	The holiness of God alongside his tenderness and love
620	ZEPHANIAH	(involved in Josiah's reforms in Judah)	Blessing after repentance is promised	The need to live morally upright lives
620	NAHUM		Message against Nineveh, which fell to the Assyrians in 612	Denunciation of ruthless military power
605	HABAKKUK		Debates justice of God in allowing the ungodly to defeat God's people	The need for continuing faithfulness to God even when it does not seem worthwhile
Begins 605	DANIEL	Daniel, his friends; Nebuchadnezzar, Belshazzar	Life in exile in Babylon; a series of prophecies about future nations	Steadfast faith despite persecution; God is in control of history
593–575	EZEKIEL		Another exile, speaking from Babylon. Visions of Judah's state; ideal worship foreseen in a new temple	God is all-powerful
580	OBADIAH		God's judgement on Edom	
538–430	EZRA NEHEMIAH	Ezra, Nehemiah	Groups of exiles return to Judah from Babylon; rebuilding of Jerusalem and its temple	God's people working against great odds

APPROX DATES OF MAIN EVENTS (BC) to which books refer (not the date of composition)	BIBLE BOOK	MAIN CHARACTERS	MAIN EVENTS/SUBJECTS	MAIN TEACHING/ RELEVANCE
520	HAGGAI ZECHARIAH		Encouragement to the returned exiles to complete the temple	Lack of spiritual life hinders national growth; visions of God's glory
465	ESTHER	Esther, King Ahasuerus, Mordecai	Life during the Persian Empire	Human story showing how God is in control of events
460	MALACHI		Morale in Jerusalem at low ebb; summons people to faith and looks forward to Day of the Lord	A challenge to faith and commitment
—	JOEL		Plague of locusts symbolises God's judgement	Looks forward to the end of time
—	PROVERBS	—	Wisdom relating to everyday life	Practical insight for godly living
—	ECCLESIASTES		A humanist view of life	Futility of life without God
—	SONG OF SOLOMON	—	A love poem	The beauty of human love
—	PSALMS	—	God's past actions; his character; human aspirations	Helps for prayer and worship
—	JOB	—	A loyal Jew refuses to be shackled by popular theology	A suffering man who retains his faith while asking searching questions

The Old Testament describes an ancient way of life but its message of God's care is timeless.

Visions of the future

From 200 BC onwards, life became hard for the Jews. They were harassed by Greek and Roman invaders, and during the reign of Antiochus Epiphanes suffered serious persecution. Furthermore, God seemed silent. There had been no prophets to bring the word of God to the people for two centuries. But hope was not utterly lost.

Apocalyptic literature

A new form of literature known as 'apocalyptic' developed in this period. The name comes from a Greek word meaning 'unveiling' or 'revelation'. Nearly twenty known documents fall under this broad heading, with a dozen more among the Dead Sea Scrolls. The books are very pessimistic about the present, but look forward to a day when God will triumph over the enemies of Israel in a spectacular way.

Apocalyptic writing is often unintelligible to modern readers because of its strange and intricate symbolism. In *Enoch*, for example, stars fall from heaven and become bulls, and all kinds of animals and mysterious beasts are described. The immediate impression of some of these visions is that they are dreams, or nightmares.

That they claim to be genuine prophetic 'visions' is undeniable, but most scholars regard them as 'pious fiction'. None of the more extravagant books was considered a genuine message from God, and was thus excluded from the collection of specially-inspired books of the Bible. They are often written under pseudonyms, the authors claiming to be great men of Israel's past, such as Enoch or Moses. They attempt to predict the future, and often write as if the alleged author were in fact looking ahead to the time in

which the books were written.

The apocalyptists are agreed that this world is evil and corrupt, and they look forward to a new age ushered in by God himself. This helped the people at the time to come to terms with their own suffering and retain their faith in a good God who would eventually triumph over evil.

Some of the Bible books belong to this form of literature, including parts of Isaiah and Ezekiel, and the books of Daniel

and Revelation. But the tone of the biblical writings is different from most other apocalyptic literature.

The Book of Ezekiel

This long book of prophecies is organized meticulously into clearly-defined sections and the main visions and prophecies carefully dated. Although it was written some time before apocalyptic literature became common, it contains strange symbolic images: wheels within

readily. He emphasized individual responsibility for wrongdoing, too, just as Jeremiah, his contemporary in Jerusalem, was doing.

And his far-reaching vision could see a time when there would be restoration for the repentant exiles, and a whole new order of life. The dry bones of Israel would be brought to life by the Spirit of God (chapter 37).

Daniel

Daniel in the lion's den is much more familiar than Ezekiel, but the book of Daniel, like Ezekiel, contains not only historical narrative but also several visions of the future.

Daniel, like Ezekiel, was taken into exile in Babylon. He was evidently a young man of promise and ability, and he rose to privilege and responsibility in Nebuchadnezzar's court. Many modern scholars reject the book's own claim to have been written at the time of these events, in the sixth century BC, and place it in the second century BC, largely because of the knowledge the prophet shows of the rise and fall of the Persian, Greek and Roman Empires. This position is not without its own difficulties, however, not least because the book of Daniel was already accepted as scripture in the second century.

Dreams play an important part in Daniel. Not only does he interpret the dreams of various kings, but he also has several dreams of his own. His visions are reflected in Jesus' teaching about the end of the world, and in the book of Revelation. The prophecies about the great statue (chapter 2) and the four beasts (chapter 7) have been taken by some to refer to the period of the Maccabees, and some to Jesus' own lifetime, but others see in them visions about the very end of time. Visions and symbols by their very nature, can be found relevant at different times.

wheels full of eyes, flashing lights and strange creatures (chapter 1). He often used visual aids, acting out his message in front of the people. Towards the end of the book is a combination of nostalgia and hope: a long, detailed plan of the ideal temple and its services (40–48).

Ezekiel was speaking to the Jews at the time of the exile. Although he had been taken to Babylon himself, many of his prophecies were directed at those who had remained in

Jerusalem. But he looked further afield, too. He tried to prepare the Jews in Babylon for the role they would have when they returned home, and he spoke against Tyre, Egypt and other Near Eastern countries.

Ezekiel saw himself as a watchman (chapter 33) with the responsibility for pointing out the coming judgement of God which he could foresee. It was an unpleasant task, but once his first prophecies came true the people listened to him more

Between the testaments

The rise of Greece

Alexander the Great was king of Greece for only thirteen years, but in that short space of time he changed the course of history, and spread Greek ideas and customs across the then-known world. He was only twenty years old when he became king of Macedon, a district in northern Greece, in the same year that Darius III became emperor of Persia.

336 BC

He soon gained control over the whole country. Then, inspired by his ambition to introduce the Greek language and culture to countries far beyond his own borders, his army of 40,000 men marched across Asia Minor. He drove south through Palestine into Egypt, where he founded a new city, Alexandria. In fact he established many new cities, and named sixteen of them Alexandria. They became important centres of Greek influence across the new empire.

The Persian Empire crumbled before him; at times he defeated armies twice as large as his own. From Egypt he marched east, capturing Babylon, Susa and Persepolis. When

Alexander the Great, from a mosaic showing his defeat of Darius and the Persians at the Battle of Issus in 333 BC.

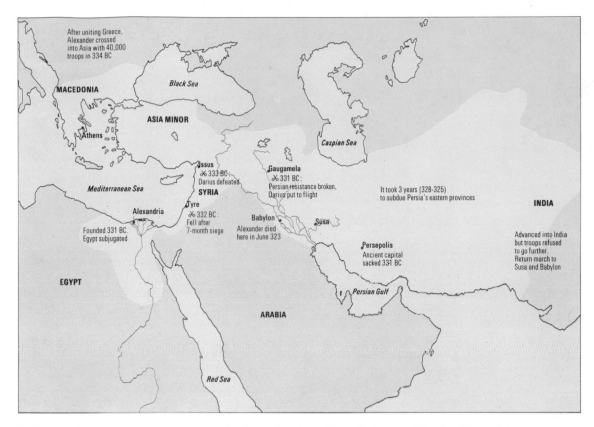

The Greek Empire

he had reached the River Indus and the foothills of the Himalayan mountains, his army decided at last that they had had enough of fighting and wanted to return home. Alexander died of a fever at Babylon on the homeward journey, having thoroughly earned his nickname, 'The Great'.

323 BC

At his death, Alexander's empire was divided among four of his generals. One of these, Seleucus, gained Mesopotamia, Asia Minor and Syria, and set up his capital at Antioch in Syria. His descendants were called 'Seleucids'. Another general, Ptolemy, became ruler of Egypt, and established the dynasty of the Ptolemies.

Judah under the Ptolemies

The land of the Jews lay in between these two great kingdoms, and the Seleucids and Ptolemies continually battled for control of Judah. From 323 to 198 BC it was ruled by the Ptolemies for most of the time. During this period people in Palestine began to adopt Greek customs and wear Greek clothes. The Greek language became more familiar. But the Ptolemies did not deliberately interfere with the Jewish way of life, and allowed the Jews to practise their religion as they wished.

Then in 198 BC, Antiochus III, a Seleucid ruler, won a decisive battle over the Egyptian forces at Paneas (later called Caesarea Philippi). The whole of Palestine now lay in Seleucid hands, and a time of testing lay ahead for the Jews.

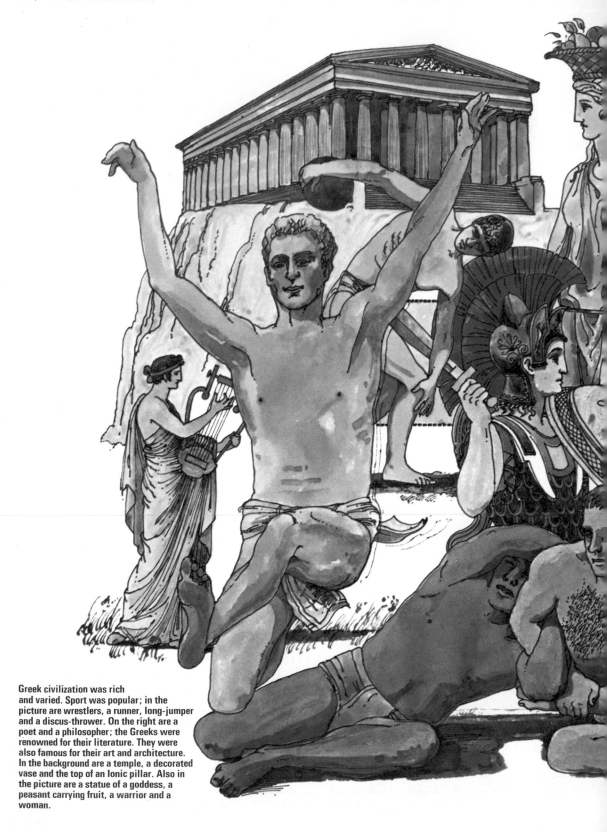

Greek civilization was rich and varied. Sport was popular; in the picture are wrestlers, a runner, long-jumper and a discus-thrower. On the right are a poet and a philosopher; the Greeks were renowned for their literature. They were also famous for their art and architecture. In the background are a temple, a decorated vase and the top of an Ionic pillar. Also in the picture are a statue of a goddess, a peasant carrying fruit, a warrior and a woman.

Judah under the Greeks
175–163 BC

During the reign of Antiochus III the Jews were left in relative peace. There seemed no cause for alarm. But his son Antiochus IV was a very different kind of ruler. He demanded that all his subjects should worship him as though he were a god. And he was determined to impose Greek customs on every nation subject to him, whether they liked it or not.

And some of them did like it. A gymnasium in the Greek style was built in Jerusalem, and Jewish young men began to go there in the typical dress of Greek youths – a broad-brimmed hat, tunic and a short riding cloak. Some of the priests were so keen on athletics that they would leave the altar of sacrifice in the temple and rush to see the discus-throwing.

But many Jews were rigidly opposed to these new developments. Athletes were forced to compete naked, which was against the Jewish law. They believed that God demanded separation from pagan customs, and feared that their young people were being led away from faith in him. The result was a split between those Jews who welcomed the new Greek influence, and those who preferred the traditional ways.

But greater problems still were to come. In 171 BC Antiochus IV (who was surnamed 'Epiphanes' which means 'God is revealed') horrified orthodox Jews by auctioning the job of high priest to the highest bidder. The buyer was a man named Menelaus, who agreed with Antiochus' plan to destroy Jewish religion and replace it with the Greek way of life. Then Antiochus attempted to deal the death-blow to Judaism. In 167 BC he issued a decree making Jewish religion illegal. Anyone who offered a sacrifice in the temple, tried to keep the Jewish law, or possessed a copy of the scriptures, was to be put to death.

Antiochus set up an altar to the chief Greek god, Zeus, in the Jerusalem temple. Jews had to show their obedience to the decree by offering sacrifice to Zeus there, or at one of the many local altars which were built elsewhere in Judea. Many faithful Jews preferred to die rather than disobey their law by worshipping false gods.

The Maccabaean Revolt

An old priest named Mattathias lived at Modein, a village 17 miles/27km north-west of Jerusalem, with his five sons. When Antiochus' official arrived to set up a pagan altar and ordered the villagers to offer sacrifice to Zeus, Mattathias refused. Another Jew stepped forward to offer the sacrifice, and Mattathias drew his sword and killed both him and the imperial official. Turning to the crowds around him he shouted, 'Whoever loves the law and stands by the covenant, follow me!' Then he fled to the hills with his sons and other supporters. So, in 167 BC, the Wars of the Maccabees began.

The most famous of Mattathias' sons was Judas. For six years he led the Jews in revolt against their Greek oppressors. They lived in the hills and made surprise attacks on Antiochus' Syrian armies. Antiochus even used elephants in his armies, but they were far too cumbersome against Judas' men, who moved about swiftly and knew the hill-country very well. Judas was so successful that he was nicknamed 'Maccabaeus', which means 'the Hammerer', and his family became known as the Maccabees.

After three years of 'hammering' the Syrian armies, Judas destroyed the altar to Zeus in the temple at Jerusalem in 164 BC. Once more the Jews were able to offer sacrifices to the God of Israel. Ever since that time the Jews have celebrated this event at their festival of 'Hanukkah' (rededication of the Temple).

Antiochus died in 163 BC. But in spite of Judas' victories Judea was still under Seleucid rule. Judas and his supporters wanted to be free from control by their pagan enemies, and fought on till they achieved this goal. Judas was killed in battle in 161 BC, but his brothers Jonathan and Simon continued the struggle. At last, in 142 BC, Simon obtained from the Seleucid king, Demetrius II, a treaty which gave the Jews political independence.

Now, for the first time since the exile over 400 years before, the Jews were governed not by foreigners but by their own leaders. Simon and his descendants were both political and religious leaders, holding the offices of both ruler (or king) and high priest.

For eighty years Judea was an independent nation. But often the country was not at peace. Some of its kings were cruel and hungry for power. During the second half of that period there were frequent civil wars. The Maccabees had fought to win political and religious freedom, but the Jews who came after them could not agree how to use this freedom. When the Romans arrived in 63 BC, their time of freedom was over. The Jews were not to govern themselves in their own country until 1948, when the modern state of Israel was established.

An isolated tank on the Golan Heights is a reminder that even today Israel is a country rarely at peace.

The conquest of Galilee

Ever since they had returned from the Babylonian exile, the Jews had been confined to a small area round Jerusalem. And during the period when the Seleucids ruled Palestine, most of the regions to the north of Judea had adopted Greek customs and spoke the Greek language. Galilee was one of these regions.

But once the Maccabees had set Judea free from the control of Syria, some of the rulers who came after them were keen to expand their territory. Aristobulus I reigned for only one year, but during that time he organized the conquest of Galilee. The non-Jews who lived there were compelled to submit to the Jewish law. And so, when Jesus began his work 130 years later, Galilee was a Jewish district.

Aristobulus: 104–103 BC

The ruler who followed Aristobulus was Alexander Jannaeus. He made more conquests, and the kingdom of Judea became nearly as big as the Israel ruled by King Solomon.

Jannaeus: 103–76 BC

The Roman influence

After eighty years of self-government, the Jews once again became subject to a foreign power – Rome. In 63 BC, the Roman general Pompey was in the Near East, subduing Syria into a province of Rome. When he received requests for help from two rival claimants to the Jewish throne, he decided to settle their argument by claiming Judea for Rome. He entered

The Roman Empire

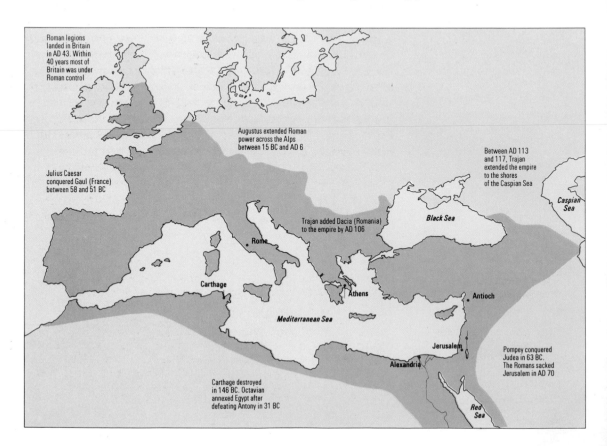

Roman legions landed in Britain in AD 43. Within 40 years most of Britain was under Roman control

Augustus extended Roman power across the Alps between 15 BC and AD 6

Between AD 113 and 117, Trajan extended the empire to the shores of the Caspian Sea

Julius Caesar conquered Gaul (France) between 58 and 51 BC

Trajan added Dacia (Romania) to the empire by AD 106

Caspian Sea

Black Sea

Rome

Carthage

Athens

Antioch

Mediterranean Sea

Jerusalem

Pompey conquered Judea in 63 BC. The Romans sacked Jerusalem in AD 70

Alexandria

Carthage destroyed in 146 BC. Octavian annexed Egypt after defeating Antony in 31 BC

Red Sea

Ostia was situated at the mouth of the River Tiber and was the ancient seaport for Rome. Founded in the seventh century BC, its greatest prosperity was in the second century AD. Land reclamation earlier this century uncovered the remains of the city.

Jerusalem, and ensured that from then on the Jews were governed only by rulers of whom Rome approved.

The city of Rome in Italy was hundreds of miles to the west of Palestine. Founded, it is thought, in 753 BC, it was originally ruled by kings, and later by a Senate of several hundred members drawn mainly from rich families. The Senate was led by two consuls, who held the post for one year. By 250 BC, Rome controlled the whole of Italy, and began to conquer other lands around the Mediterranean Sea. But to conquer and control territory, the Romans needed bigger and bigger armies. Consequently, army generals became very powerful, and it soon became possible for them to march on Rome itself, with an army behind them, and overthrow the government.

So, in the first century BC, there were numerous civil wars and much political uncertainty. Julius Caesar, Pompey and Mark Antony were battling with each other for power. In the end, Julius Caesar's adopted son, Octavian, managed to defeat

The Jewish 'Dispersion'

Ever since the Jews were deported to Babylon, large numbers of them have lived outside Palestine. Many Jews remained in Babylon, even though Cyrus encouraged them to go home to Judah. And already there were Jews living in Egypt.

As time went on, Jews settled in many other cities around the Mediterranean. They were called 'The Dispersion' (which means 'scattered'). By the time of Jesus there were more Jews living outside Palestine than in it. Paul often went to Jewish communities on his missionary journeys.

Today, many Jews have gone back to live in Israel. But there are still far more Jews in other countries, mostly in Europe and North America, than there are in Israel.

his rivals and win the support of the Roman people. In 27 BC, he took the title Augustus and was acclaimed emperor – supreme ruler – of Rome and its provinces.

Augustus was a good ruler and was welcomed as one who brought peace. He reorganized the government of the provinces. He allowed the Senate to appoint governors of the older, more settled provinces, such as Sicily, where no armies were stationed. But the newer provinces, where there was more danger of revolt or attack from across the frontiers, were ruled by governors personally appointed by the emperor. And in these provinces the Roman legions maintained law and order.

Luke 2:1; 3:1

Augustus reigned until his death in AD 14, and was succeeded by his stepson Tiberius, who ruled till AD 37. Jesus' life fell within the reigns of these two emperors.

The Jews and Rome

Although Palestine was under Roman rule from 63 BC, the Roman government allowed the Jews to be ruled by local kings. The most famous of these was Herod the Great, who ruled Judea, Samaria and Galilee. By bold scheming he had won the support of various influential Romans, and was a personal friend of Augustus.

Herod was hated by many Jews because he was only half-Jewish; his ancestors were Idumeans (Edomites) from the area south of Judea. He tried to win their approval by rebuilding the temple in Jerusalem, and he

certainly succeeded in making it grander and more beautiful than ever. He also secured for Jews of the Dispersion the right to contribute to the temple treasury in Jerusalem, and exemption from service in the Roman army. Military service would have made it necessary for them to break laws governing the sabbath.

However, Herod's building projects also included temples in honour of Augustus at Paneas (later called Caesarea Philippi), Sebaste (formerly Samaria) and Caesarea (the magnificent new city which he built on the coast), which did not endear him to orthodox Jews.

Above: a Roman standard-bearer.

Right: Roman bakers and cooks prepare a meal for the family who are seated at the table.

Herod was ruthless with people he suspected of being hostile towards him. He put to death several of his own family, fearing that they were trying to take over his throne. This state of affairs provoked Augustus' famous remark, that it would be safer to be one of Herod's pigs than one of his sons!

When Herod died in 4 BC his kingdom was divided among three of his sons. Archelaus got Judea, Idumea and Samaria, Herod Antipas became tetrarch ('ruler of a fourth part') of Galilee and Perea, and Herod Philip tetrarch of Gaulanitis, Iturea and Trachonitis.

Almost immediately there were uprisings in Judea, Perea and Galilee by Jews hoping to throw off the rule of Rome and of Herod's family. Varus, governor of the Roman province of Syria, moved in swiftly with three legions to crush the rebellion. About two thousand Jewish rebels were punished by crucifixion.

In AD 6 Augustus deposed Archelaus and made his territory into a Roman province, named Judea. Its governor (known as *praefectus* or *procurator*) was directly responsible to the emperor. A census was organized to determine what taxes should now be paid to Rome. Even though the new taxes were to be paid only by inhabitants of Judea, there arose in Galilee another revolutionary movement, led by two men from a Pharisaic background, Judas and Zadok. Once again, the rebellion was put down, and the leaders were killed. But many Jews continued to cherish the hope that they would be able, like the Maccabees in an earlier period, to defeat their foreign rulers and to make their nation free again.

In particular, they resented paying taxes to Rome. And they hated the interference in their religious life which some of the Roman governors attempted. Pontius Pilate, governor of Judea, for example, tactlessly sent troops into Jerusalem carrying standards bearing a picture of the emperor's head, though this was against the Jewish law which forbade 'graven images'. Later he used temple money to improve the water supply to Jerusalem. This provoked rioting, which Pilate squashed violently. Finally, he massacred some Samaritans involved in a messianic movement. For this he was removed from office by the governor of Syria, acting on

Right: a victorious Roman charioteer.

Below: soldiers building a fortress, shown on part of the Trajan Column in Rome.

instructions of the Emperor Tiberius.

The Zealot movement (so-called because of their zeal for God and for Judaism) developed out of this turmoil. Sometimes the anti-Roman feeling broke out into open rebellion. In AD 41–44 there was a brief rest from direct Roman rule, since the new emperor Claudius made Herod Agrippa I, grandson of Herod the Great, king over all his grandfather's territory. But after Claudius' death, Roman procurators were once again appointed – this time over Galilee as well as Judea and Samaria. And events began to move towards a climax. Support for the Zealots steadily increased. They began to go about with daggers under their cloaks, and to kill fellow-Jews whom they suspected of being friendly with the Romans, or of rejecting Jewish traditions.

The defeat of the Jews

In AD 66 the last procurator, Gessius Florus, demanded a huge payment from the temple treasury. This led to anti-Roman demonstrations, and daily sacrifices on behalf of the emperor ceased in the temple. This was an official declaration of rebellion. As well as Zealots, the rebels included loyal aristocratic families. They were supported by the people of Judea, Idumea, Galilee and Perea, but not Samaria.

Roman legions marched south from Syria and occupied northern Jerusalem, but could not capture the temple area. The Emperor Nero appointed Vespasian to organize the campaign against the Jewish rebels. With sixty thousand troops, he had re-captured all the rebels' territory by AD 68, except for the area around Jerusalem itself, and some fortresses near the Dead Sea.

Right: a Roman legionary.

Below: a present-day occupation force – Russian tanks in Prague, Czechoslovakia.

Vespasian's attack on Jerusalem was delayed, because disturbances in Rome had brought Nero's reign to an end. In 68–69 three men battled for power, each ruling briefly as emperor, only to be ousted by his successor. Then came a fourth, Vespasian himself, who left his son Titus to complete the siege of Jerusalem and ruled as emperor from AD 69 to 79.

The Jewish forces were greatly weakened through disputes and fighting among themselves. Against the four legions of Titus, they could hardly hope to survive. Their leaders John of Gischala and Simon bar Giora led a brave fight, so that it took four months for the Romans to capture the temple area. On 10 August, AD 70, the temple of Herod – which had only been completed in 63 – was destroyed by fire. A month later the upper city, south-west of the temple, fell to the Romans, and John and Simon perished.

Not till AD 73 was Jewish resistance finally crushed, however, after the famous last stand of the Zealots at Masada near the Dead Sea. Defeat in this war meant the end of the Jewish state. The Sanhedrin and high priesthood were abolished, and temple worship ceased. But Judaism survived through the energy of the Pharisaic scribes or rabbis, who continued to interpret the law and to apply it to the new situation of their people.

THE BIRTH OF CHRISTIANITY

For 500 years, the Jews had rarely been their own masters in the land of Israel. Even when King Cyrus of Persia had released them from captivity in Babylonia, they were soon subject to the Greeks, and then the Romans. The nation groaned under the burden of taxes paid to a foreign power and of being forced to take part in activities reflecting an alien culture. During the 200 years before Christ came stirrings of hope for a messiah who would deliver them from the oppressor. But when Jesus was born, he was not recognized as the deliverer he later claimed to be. He was crucified as a blasphemer, for he claimed to be able to release people from the greater oppression of their own failure to live as God had intended they should. But from that event has sprung the Christian faith, and the claim that Jesus, though crucified, still lives on.

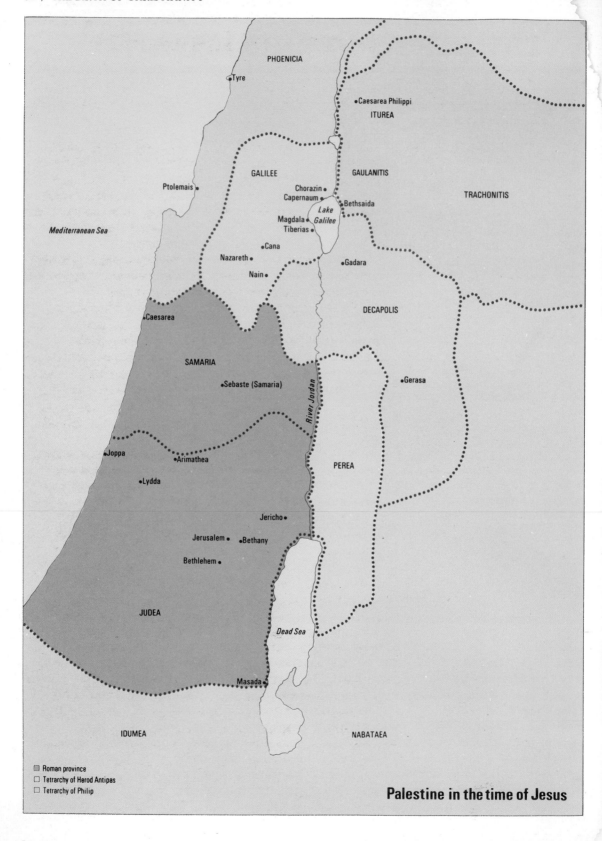

PHOENICIA

• Tyre

• Caesarea Philippi

ITUREA

GALILEE

GAULANITIS

TRACHONITIS

Ptolemais •

Chorazin •
Capernaum •
• Bethsaida

Lake Galilee

Magdala •
Tiberias •

Mediterranean Sea

• Cana

Nazareth •

• Gadara

Nain •

DECAPOLIS

• Caesarea

SAMARIA

• Sebaste (Samaria)

River Jordan

• Gerasa

• Joppa

• Arimathea

PEREA

• Lydda

Jericho •

Jerusalem • • Bethany

Bethlehem •

JUDEA

Dead Sea

• Masada

IDUMEA

NABATAEA

☐ Roman province
☐ Tetrarchy of Herod Antipas
☐ Tetrarchy of Philip

Palestine in the time of Jesus

Jesus and his world

Jesus' birth

Nazareth in the time of the Emperor Augustus was a small and unimportant town in the district of Galilee. It was hardly the sort of place one would expect to find a young man who in later centuries would be worshipped by hundreds of millions of people. But Nazareth was the home of Joseph and Mary, who had come to believe that Mary would become the mother of the Jews' long-awaited saviour – their messiah.

Luke 2:1

While she was waiting for her baby to be born, Augustus ordered a census to be taken. It seems that this counting of the people took place every fourteen years, so that the government could work out what taxes were due from the people. Because of the census Joseph had to go back to the place where his family came from. So he travelled to Bethlehem, 85 miles/135km to the south, taking Mary with him. Because Bethlehem was crowded with people who had come for the census, Joseph and Mary had to stay in a cave or an

Luke 2:7

outhouse behind an inn. And while they were there, Mary gave birth to a son, and laid him in a manger. The baby was named Jesus, which means 'God saves'.

Matthew 1:21

Although the importance of his birth passed unnoticed by most people, Jesus was visited at Bethlehem by 'wise men' from the east. These were probably astrologers from Persia who studied the stars and believed that unusual events in the heavens were signs that important events were about to happen on earth. The 'star' which they saw may have been the planets Jupiter and Saturn, in the constellation of Pisces, coming close together, and so causing a very bright light. In ancient thinking Jupiter was the royal star belonging to the ruler of gods and men, and Saturn was the star of Israel. So it is not surprising that these astrologers came to Jerusalem to look for a new world ruler. This coming together of Jupiter and Saturn took place in 7 BC, and only occurs every 794 years.

Another theory suggested by some astronomers is that the star was a 'nova', a short-lived but brilliant flare caused by the explosion of a white dwarf star. According to Chinese records, a nova appeared in the eastern sky in 5 BC. The actual year of Jesus' birth is unclear. An error by a monk who was commissioned by Pope Gregory to draw up the modern calendar in the ninth century, has been discovered. Jesus' birth probably took place around 4 or 5 BC, not 1 AD as the monk calculated.

On arrival at Jerusalem the astrologers were informed that,

according to Old Testament prophecy, God's promised messiah was to be born at Bethlehem, 6 miles/10km south of Jerusalem. So at Bethlehem they found Jesus, and brought him their gifts. But Herod, always fearful that someone might try to take his throne from him, was determined to make sure that this new 'king' did not become a rival to his authority, and ordered all boys under two years old in Bethlehem to be killed. Joseph and Mary, however, had already fled with Jesus south to Egypt, which lay well outside the territory governed by Herod.

Matthew 2:19-23

When Herod the Great died in 4 BC, his kingdom was divided among his sons. Joseph was now ready to take his family back to Palestine. But knowing that Archelaus, the new ruler of Judea, was as cruel as his father had been, Joseph decided to avoid Judea and returned north to Nazareth. But not long afterwards, in AD 6, Archelaus was deposed by Augustus, who officially declared Judea a Roman province, and placed it under the control of a Roman governor, known as a *praefectus*.

Jesus in Nazareth

Nazareth, where Jesus grew up, was a town nestling in the hills of Galilee. But it was not an isolated place. From the hills Jesus could look southwards to the fertile plain of Jezreel, scene of several battles fought in Old Testament times. Now he could watch traders and travellers crossing the plain on the main road which led from Mesopotamia down to the Mediterranean coast and eventually to Egypt.

A typical small family house in first-century Palestine. The animals are housed downstairs, where the kitchen and workshops are situated. The family lives upstairs, and often uses the roof as an extra room.

A child watches the family's animals drinking outside a peasant home near the Mount of Olives.

Also nearby were main roads to the ports of Caesarea and Ptolemais, and to the non-Jewish area of Decapolis, on the eastern side of the Jordan Valley. Roman soldiers, too, would use these roads – a constant reminder that Palestine was a land occupied by a foreign power. And a few miles to the east was Lake Galilee, with several thriving fishing towns on its shores.

Mark 6:3

Jesus is said to have had four younger brothers and at least two sisters. At home, Joseph would tell the family about the history of the people of Israel and God's love for them. And on the sabbath, the Saturday, Jesus would go to the synagogue to worship God and to hear the Old Testament read and explained.

As well as being a place of worship, the synagogue was also a school where, from the age of five to thirteen, Jesus would go with his friends. There he would learn to read and to study the scriptures. And since Jesus' everyday language was Aramaic, he would have to learn Hebrew, in which the Old Testament was written.

Since Joseph was a carpenter, Jesus naturally learnt this trade. Joseph seems to have died while Jesus was in his teens, and Jesus must have worked hard to support the large family. But he knew that God was calling him to something different.

Luke 2:49

Even when he was only twelve years old, he told his parents that he had lingered in the temple at Jerusalem in order to 'be in my Father's house', meaning God rather than Joseph.

Jesus the teacher in Galilee

For many years the Jews had been expecting a 'messiah'. He would be a special messenger from God who would lead the people into a new freedom. Most people thought of this freedom as release from the power of the Romans who were occupying Israel at the time. At last, in about AD 27, the prophet John the Baptizer began preaching that the messiah was coming.

Large crowds came to hear him beside the River Jordan. He called people to turn away from their old self-centred ways of life and to prepare for the promised messiah. As a sign that they had turned to a new way of living, they were baptized in the river.

Matthew 3:13-17

Jesus, too, came for baptism. At that moment he heard a voice telling him that he was the promised messiah, and that he had been sent by God to bring people closer to God.

Matthew 4:1-11

Jesus then went by himself into the desert north of the Dead Sea. He spent forty days there facing in advance the problem of what form his work should take. He was tempted to win men by the spectacular demonstration of supernatural powers, or by military conquest. But he knew that this was not the way God had chosen for him. People's basic need was not deliverance from the Romans. It was a far more radical deliverance: from the vicious circle of evil, sin and death.

The western shores of the Dead Sea, looking north to Qumran, where the Dead Sea Scrolls were found.

Journeys of Jesus

John's Gospel tells us that Jesus sometimes travelled south to Jerusalem during his ministry. On one journey back from Jerusalem to Galilee, he passed through Samaria, and talked with a woman at the well in Sychar, which was also known as Shechem. Strict Jews despised the Samaritans, who were not of pure Jewish descent, and they even hated to travel through Samaritan territory. But in his actions and words Jesus showed that God loves all men equally, and many of the people of Sychar welcomed him as their messiah (John 4).

When opposition to Jesus grew in Galilee, he withdrew northwards with his disciples to the Gentile region of Tyre and Sidon in Phoenicia. During this period of withdrawal, Jesus visited Caesarea Philippi, 26 miles/42km north of Capernaum. There he asked his disciples the great question, 'Who do you say that I am?' And Peter replied, 'You are the messiah' (Mark 8:29). Now that Jesus was sure that his disciples understood who he was, he began to tell them what lay ahead. He warned them that he would be rejected by the religious leaders, and be put to death. But after three days, he would rise from death (Mark 8:31).

One of the sources of the River Jordan at Caesarea Philippi (modern Banias).

What was needed was a new start, a new way of life, a whole new creation.

Matthew 4:17   So Jesus began to preach about the new kingdom of God. The Old Testament prophets had looked forward to the time when God would act powerfully to set up his kingly rule. Now, said Jesus, the time had arrived. But it was not to be seen in military victories. Rather, it was demonstrated in works of healing, in God's forgiveness offered to all who were **Luke 4:18**   conscious of their need of it: 'He has anointed me to preach good news to the poor.'

Jesus began his work in Judea, near where John had baptized him. But he soon went back to Galilee, where he quickly attracted followers in villages beside the lake. The centre of his activity was Capernaum, but we are also told about Magdala (where Mary Magdalene came from), **Mark 6:30-44**   Bethsaida Julias, where Jesus fed 5,000 people from five loaves and two fishes, and Chorazin, whose inhabitants refused to follow Jesus even though they witnessed his teaching and miracles. And in the hills near Nazareth there were villages **Luke 7:11-17**   such as Nain, where Jesus restored a dead boy to life, and **John 2:1-11**   Cana where he changed water into wine at a wedding celebration.

The Gospels do not tell us in detail the order of events in Jesus' ministry or the exact routes which he travelled. Instead they record incidents in his life as examples of his teaching **Luke 6:12-16**   and healing, loving and caring. From his first followers he

Working life in Palestine

The farmer

The main grain crops were wheat and barley, which were used for making bread. When Jesus fed 5,000 people, he used two fish and five barley-loaves offered by a small boy (John 6:1-13).

The farmer sowed the seed for his cereal crops in November or December, after the autumn rains had softened the ground. Some farmers ploughed up the soil before sowing; others sowed first and then ploughed the seed into the ground. They used wooden ploughs pulled by oxen. More rain during winter and spring helped the crops grow, until they were harvested between March and May.

The farmer reaped the crop with a sickle. The corn was then carried to a hard, flat piece of ground used as a threshing-floor. There the grain was separated from the straw either by oxen treading it or by a wooden sledge pulled by oxen.

The next job was winnowing. The farmer threw the threshed corn into the air with a pitchfork, and the breeze would carry away the light husks while the heavier grain fell back on the floor. The grain could then be sifted and bagged, ready to be ground into flour for bread-making.

Other crops were flax, grapes, figs and olives. Flax was used for making linen clothes. Grapes were crushed to make wine. Fig-trees were a major source of fruit. Olives were eaten fresh or pickled, and were also crushed in a press to produce olive oil, which was used for cooking, medicine, and as fuel for lamps.

The carpenter

Joseph and Jesus were carpenters. As well as making beds, tables and chairs, they also built and repaired houses. They made ploughs, yokes to go across the necks of oxen pulling ploughs, and threshing instruments for farmers to use. The tools which carpenters used

Above: a stonemason.

Far right: a builder draws up his plans and a tentmaker sews skins together.

included the saw made of iron and the chisel made of copper. The bow-drill, which has a copper bit, is still used today in the East.

The fisherman

There was a busy fishing industry on Lake Galilee. Many fish were pickled and exported as far as Rome. Several of Jesus' disciples were fishermen.

The Lake today contains about twenty-four different kinds of fish, including carp, a small lake sardine, and a fish known as St Peter's Fish. This fish has a large mouth, in which it carries its eggs. It could have held the coin which Peter found in a fish's mouth (see Matthew 17:27).

Fish were sometimes caught with a hook and line, but usually a net was used. Peter and Andrew were using a casting net when Jesus met them (Matthew 4:18). The fisherman stands in shallow water and throws the net over the water. Weights round its edge make it sink, trapping fish underneath.

A larger net, called a drag-net, is let down from boats. The fish caught in it are hauled into the boat (Luke 5:7), or else dragged to the shore (Matthew 13:48; John 21:8). Fishing was often done at night (Luke 5:5; John 21:3); night fishing is common today in Galilee.

The shepherd

Sheep were kept both in Galilee and in Judea. Bethlehem, where Jesus was born, was an important sheep-rearing district. The shepherd made sure his sheep had enough to eat, and sometimes he would have to walk a long way with them to find suitable grazing land. He also protected them from wild animals, such as wolves and jackals. At night he would collect them together in a pen made of dry-stone walls. He would lie across the entrance to protect the sheep from predators and thieves.

Often sheep and goats were kept together in the same flock. Goats were not as valuable as sheep, but they could provide up to three litres of milk a day. Sheep's wool was good for clothing, goats' hair was woven to make tents, and both animals provided meat. Both were also used for sacrifices in the temple at Jerusalem.

Fishermen mend their nets at Tiberias, on Lake Galilee.

Luke 4:16-30

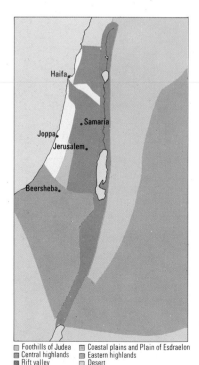

Israel: physical regions

- ☐ Foothills of Judea
- ☐ Central highlands
- ☐ Rift valley
- ☐ Coastal plains and Plain of Esdraelon
- ☐ Eastern highlands
- ☐ Desert

chose twelve disciples, the apostles, to share in his work.

Nazareth itself gave Jesus a hostile reception. The people there remembered him as the son of Joseph the carpenter. But when he spoke in the synagogue he made the dramatic claim that he was the messiah who had come to deliver both Jews and non-Jews. They ran him out of town to throw him over a cliff. But Jesus escaped and returned to Capernaum.

As time went on the opposition to Jesus increased. Although he was clearly a good man, some people hated him. He taught that God cares for non-Jews (or Gentiles, as they were called), contrary to the common belief of the time that the Jews alone were God's chosen people. That idea was very offensive to many Jews.

Jesus also accused the Jewish religious teachers of making it hard for ordinary people to do God's will because they had added hundreds of extra rules to the Old Testament law. The religious leaders in turn accused Jesus of breaking the rules they had made. For example, they said that it was wrong to heal someone on the day of rest, the sabbath. To them, healing was a form of work, and to work on the sabbath was forbidden.

There was also a third type of opposition. Many people who at first had hoped that Jesus would deliver them from the Romans became bitter when they realized that he was not interested in military power. He was not the kind of messiah they had expected.

Opposition increased. So, too, did Jesus' determination to continue with this ministry. And as he did so, he also began to speak of the death he would have to die.

The road to Jerusalem

Jesus frequently told his disciples that he would eventually have to go to Jerusalem for the last time, when he would be betrayed and executed. They did not understand what he meant; they were carried along on a wave of success and popularity. But after about three years' teaching and travelling, he journeyed with his disciples down the east side of the Jordan, southwards to Jericho and from there to Jerusalem.

The road passed near the villages of Bethany and Bethphage on the Mount of Olives. From one of these villages Jesus borrowed a donkey and rode it down the slopes of the Mount of Olives into Jerusalem. He was fulfilling the prophecy of Zechariah that the messiah would enter Jerusalem 'humble, and mounted on a donkey'. A military ruler would have chosen to ride a horse; by choosing a donkey Jesus showed that his purpose was one of peace and love. As he rode, crowds welcomed him enthusiastically, and threw clothes and leafy branches in his path, shouting, 'Hosanna! Blessed is he who comes in the name of the Lord!'

The next day Jesus went again into the city and drove the traders and money changers out of the temple area, declaring

Mark 11:1-10

Zechariah 9:9

Mark 11:15-19

Each Good Friday a procession in Jerusalem follows the 'Via Dolorosa' or 'Way of Sorrows' – the route traditionally believed to be that taken by Jesus on his way to crucifixion.

that God's house of prayer had been turned into a robbers' den. For the religious authorities this was the last straw. During the next two or three days, which Jesus spent teaching in the city, they laid plans to arrest him. On the Thursday night, they seized their opportunity.

Matthew 26:20-25 Jesus had spent the evening eating the 'last supper' with his disciples. During the meal Judas slipped away to tell the authorities where Jesus could be arrested without any risk that crowds of Jesus' supporters would be present. Jesus and the other disciples sang a psalm together and then walked across the Kidron Valley to the secluded Garden of Gethsemane on the slopes of the Mount of Olives. There he committed his work to God in prayer with great anguish as he thought of the suffering he would experience. And there the arrest was made.

Matthew 26:57–27:26 An illegal trial was held; it contravened the Jews' own laws by being held at night. First there was an informal examination at the high priest's house, then a formal meeting of the Sanhedrin (the Jewish Council of Elders). They convicted him of blasphemy because he claimed to have a unique relationship with God. But they had no power to put people to death; only the Roman authorities could do that. So in the early morning they brought Jesus before the Roman governor,

The synagogue

The centre of Jewish worship was the temple at Jerusalem, where animals were sacrificed on the altar and the priests performed their service to God. But because not all Jews could get to the temple very often, synagogues were built where they could meet for worship. The synagogue was also a centre of primary education and social life. The New Testament refers to synagogues at several places including Capernaum, Nazareth, and Corinth. They began during the Jewish exile in Babylon, when of course the temple had been destroyed.

No sacrifices took place in the synagogues. Instead, prayers were said every day, in both the morning and evening. And at the sabbath-day service the people said prayers, sang psalms, and heard readings from the law (the first five books of the Old Testament) and from the books of the prophets. After the readings, someone would explain their meaning to the people.

When Jesus visited the synagogue at Nazareth shortly after his baptism he was invited to read from the scriptures. He read from Isaiah 61 which promised that one day God would send a messiah to bring his blessings to the people. Jesus astonished everyone by claiming to be the messiah whom God had promised.

Jesus was based in Capernaum for much of his ministry. The ruins of its synagogue (right) probably date from the second century AD.

Pontius Pilate, who had come from his headquarters at Caesarea to be in Jerusalem. It was Passover time, a major Jewish festival for which thousands of people would trek to Jerusalem in order to celebrate it at the religious and civic capital of their nation.

Even though the Jewish leaders argued that Jesus was trying to start a revolution against Rome, Pilate was reluctant to condemn him to death. Learning that Jesus was a Galilean, Pilate sent him to Herod Antipas, king of Galilee and Perea, who was also staying in Jerusalem for the festival. Herod tried to question Jesus, but when he remained silent, mocked him, and then sent him back to Pilate. Not wanting to be unpopular with the Jewish leaders, Pilate ordered Jesus to be crucified, the usual Roman method of execution for those who were not Roman citizens.

Luke 23:6-12

So Jesus was hung on a cross, between two thieves, at a place called Golgotha. Within six hours he was dead from exposure and exhaustion. Joseph of Arimathea, a member of the Sanhedrin who had not voted for Jesus' execution, was allowed to take his body from the cross and place it in a tomb cut out of a rocky hillside.

Mark 15:25-39

Luke 23:50-56

The resurrection

To Jesus' closest followers his death seemed to spell defeat for all their hopes. Two unnamed disciples walking home to Emmaus from Jerusalem summed up all their disappointment: 'We had hoped that he was the one to redeem Israel!' But while Christianity has always revered the cross as the symbol of Jesus' execution, something else changed the disciples from despair to courage. Three days after the death of Jesus the tomb was empty. Then the disciples began to meet him again, risen from the dead. Within two months of the crucifixion, they were boldly proclaiming that Jesus was alive. And they were prepared to suffer – and even die – for their beliefs.

Luke 24:21

Christianity hangs or falls on the resurrection of Jesus. Paul went so far as to say that 'if Christ has not been raised, then our preaching is in vain and your faith is in vain. We are even found to be misrepresenting God, because we testified of God that he raised Christ'. Although such an event seems at first sight impossible, there are several reasons why it is considered the best interpretation of the evidence.

1 Corinthians 15:14,15

First, the Jewish authorities were never able to produce the body of Jesus, nor to convict anyone of its theft, however hard they tried. Second, the number of followers of Jesus was too great for there not to be another Judas among them, who would, under torture or threat of death, have given away such a secret if there had been one. Nor would Jesus' disciples have died for what they knew to be a false claim. Third, the appearances of Jesus have the marks of authenticity about them. They are unlike hallucinations or illusions, because they happened only for a short time, and on one occasion at least

1 Corinthians 15:6 Jesus was seen by over 500 people at the same time – hallucinations are usually very individual and personal.

As time went on, the first Christians began to understand Jesus' death and resurrection as the central acts of God in his plan to bring new life and hope to mankind. And it was this that impelled them to travel across the whole of the then-known world with the 'good news' of Jesus. The work of the Christian church had begun.

The tomb of Jesus

After Jesus' death, his body was anointed with oil and tightly wrapped in linen garments covered in perfume, in accordance with Jewish custom. It was placed in a newly-cut tomb belonging to Joseph of Arimathea. We do not know where this tomb was, but several dating from Jesus' time have been found, providing a clear idea of what his tomb was like.

Cut into the limestone of a hillside there was a room with a ledge round it where mourners could sit. An inner room led off this, with shelves or niches on which bodies were laid. Often there were several niches so that more

than one body could be buried in the same tomb. After the burial a large, round, flat stone was placed over the entrance to keep out animals and thieves. It would take several strong men to roll it back.

Right: a rock tomb near Haifa, Israel.

Below: an artist's impression of the interior of a first-century tomb.

Josephus, historian of the Jews

Apart from the Bible, the most important source of information about the history of the Jews is Josephus. Born of a priestly family in AD 37–38, he studied the traditions of Judaism carefully as he grew up, and joined the party of the Pharisees when he was nineteen.

On a visit to Rome in AD 63 he was impressed by the power of the empire. When the Jewish War with Rome broke out in AD 66 he wanted to remain neutral, fearing that the Jewish rebels stood no chance against the might of Rome. But he was persuaded to become a leader of the freedom-fighters in Galilee. He commanded the defence of Jotapata, a fortress 10 miles/ 15km north of Nazareth, which fell to the Romans in 67.

Although the survivors of the siege had made a pact to kill each other in case of defeat, Josephus and another person – the last two survivors – decided to surrender to the Romans. When he was brought before the Roman commander Vespasian, Josephus had the presence of mind to predict that Vespasian would become emperor. So Vespasian kept him prisoner, and when the prophecy came true in 69 Josephus was set free. Gratefully, he adopted the new emperor's family name, Flavius.

The following year he accompanied Titus (Vespasian's son and successor as commander of the Judean campaign) at the siege of Jerusalem. He acted as interpreter when Titus tried to offer terms to the defenders of the city. When Jerusalem fell, he obtained the freedom of many of the Jewish prisoners, including his own brother. Josephus lived until at least AD 100.

Naturally, Jewish patriots hated him for going over to the Romans. But he did them a valuable service after the war by writing books which explained their history and religion to educated citizens of the empire.

His *History of the Jewish War*, completed within a few years of the war, begins with a survey of Jewish history from 175 BC, including the Wars of the Maccabees. It then records in vivid and gruesome detail the events of the war in AD 66–70, and the mopping-up operations such as the siege of the Zealot stronghold of Masada in 73. Much of Josephus' account is based on his personal experiences of the war; he had taken notes even while on active service. Sometimes his reporting is biased, because he wanted to preserve his own reputation, or because he disliked other personalities involved in the war. But it is still an important source of information, as well as being very readable.

In 93–94 he published a much longer work, *The Antiquities of the Jews*. This is a history of the Jews (beginning in fact from the creation of the world!) down to AD 66. This mostly follows the Old Testament account, but offers important information on the period after the rise of Alexander the Great. When he comes to the first century AD, Josephus has passages about John the Baptizer, James the brother of Jesus, and even Jesus himself (*Antiquities* 18.5.2; 20.9.1; 18.3.3). In the book he wanted particularly to show the Roman aristocracy that the Jews were a noble people, with high moral standards and a remarkable history and culture.

Josephus also wrote two smaller books. *Against Apion* is a defence of his people against the attacks of Apion, a schoolteacher in Alexandria. For one thing, Josephus argued, the Jews can boast a greater antiquity as a nation than the Greeks. In his *Autobiography* he defends his own war record against the blackening of his character by another writer, Justus of Tiberias. Justus had also taken part in the Jewish revolt, had been condemned to death by Vespasian and later set free. Like Josephus, he wrote an account of the history of Israel and of the Jewish War. Clearly there was no love lost between them!

Jewish wars in biblical times are recorded in detail by the historian Josephus. This memorial in the Golan Heights recalls the Yom Kippur War of 1973.

Taxation in Judea

All Jewish men over twenty were expected to pay an annual *temple tax* which was used to maintain the temple and its services – including paying for animals slaughtered in sacrifice. In Jesus' time it was a half-shekel, but it could also be paid in a Greek silver coin of the same value, the didrachma (Matthew 17:24).

They were also required to pay the *priests' tithe* (one per cent of the produce of their land) and the *second tithe*. This tithe had to be spent in Jerusalem; the owner either brought the tithe in kind to Jerusalem, or sold it and brought the money to spend. So it was not a tax which had to be paid to someone else, but it contributed to the prosperity of Jerusalem. Since these Jewish taxes were not compulsory, it seems that many Jews did not bother to pay them; there are frequent reports of the priests being hard up.

On top of this the Romans demanded taxes too, and that is what angered the Jews. Their taxes were of two kinds.

First, there were direct taxes, usually collected by Roman officials themselves. A *land tax* amounted to nearly a quarter of what a person's land produced, and a *money and property tax* varied according to a man's wealth. Regular censuses were held to fix the amount due.

The second kind was indirect taxation, rather like modern customs duties. There were *import and export duties* of five per cent, *road-tolls*, and *sales taxes* imposed when slaves, farm produce and other articles were sold in the market. Every five years the right to collect these taxes was auctioned in Rome to finance companies, who in turn employed local men to collect the taxes for them. These local tax-collectors are called 'publicans' (from Latin *publicani*) in old versions of the English Bible. They included such men as Matthew (Levi) who collected taxes at Capernaum (Mark 2:13-14), and Zacchaeus at Jericho (Luke 19:1-10).

The Jews hated paying taxes to a foreign power. The Pharisees who tried to trap Jesus with the question, 'Is it lawful to pay taxes to Caesar?' (Mark 12:13-17), certainly objected to paying them. And all Roman taxes had to be paid in Roman coinage, which carried a picture of the emperor's head. This offended against the Jewish law which forbade the use of 'graven images'. The tax-collectors themselves were despised partly because they were considered traitors, and partly because their income came from taxes unjustly collected in excess of the Roman levy (see Luke 3:13; 19:8).

Traders and customers in the market at Nazareth.

The first Christians

With Jesus' body safely in the tomb, guarded by soldiers, his enemies could breathe a sigh of relief. The trouble and disruption he had caused, with crowds following him, some even worshipping him, was over. Yet a few weeks later the once-fearful disciples were boldly proclaiming that their leader had risen from the dead and was indeed the messiah. Such was their zeal and energy that they were later described Acts 17:6 as those who had turned the world upside-down – except that they probably considered they were turning it the right way up, as they called people back to faith and trust in God.

The Acts of the Apostles, the record of the early exploits of the small group of dedicated men and women, was written by Luke, whose earlier volume described the life of Jesus and is now one of the four Gospels. He was a companion of Paul on some of his journeys, and has been shown to have been scrupulously accurate in writing his history.

The church is born

His narrative opens with the eleven disciples (Judas, who betrayed Jesus, having committed suicide) meeting regularly with about 100 other close followers of Jesus. Peter, despite his loss of nerve after Jesus' death, had recovered his faith after seeing Jesus alive again by the shores of Galilee, and was now the leader of the group.

Seven weeks after Jesus had died, and about a week after the ascension, when he disappeared from the disciples' view for good, was the Jewish feast of Pentecost. It was the Jewish 'harvest festival' when they thanked God for his gifts of food and drink. The first Christians found they had something else to thank God for, as they met in Jerusalem once more.

Acts 2:1-4 As they prayed, they were suddenly conscious of the power of God – the Holy Spirit – filling their lives with a new dedication and, more important, a new ability to serve God and proclaim the message of Jesus. They described their experience as being like 'the rush of a mighty wind' and 'flames of fire'. Immediately their fear of being arrested by the Jewish leaders was overcome, and Peter preached to the Acts 2:14-47 crowds who had gathered in the city for the festival. 'God', he said, 'has proved that Jesus is his messiah by raising him from death. And now he offers to all men forgiveness for their wrongdoings, and a new life in friendship with the risen Jesus.' That day, says Luke, 3,000 people believed Peter's message and joined the church.

Herod the Great founded the city of Caesarea in about 22 BC, naming it in honour of the emperor, Caesar Augustus. The original theatre there dated from the Herodian period but was rebuilt during the second and third centuries AD. Caesarea became an important centre of the early Christians in Palestine.

The church begins to grow

Many of those who listened to Peter were Jewish visitors from outside Palestine. They returned home with the news that God had now spoken to men in a new way through the coming of Jesus. Right from the start, Christians began to tell the good news about Jesus to others, and their numbers grew rapidly.

Acts 2–5

At first the message was preached only to Jews, and Luke recounts Peter's preaching in Jerusalem. For a while the Christians also continued to worship at the temple, and had no desire to be different from other Jews. But then Stephen, a Greek-speaking Jew who had settled in Jerusalem and become a Christian, began to preach about Jesus. He accused the Jews of disobeying God throughout their history. Their greatest act of disobedience, he said, was to murder Jesus, God's messiah. This was more than the Jewish leaders could take, and they rushed him out of the city and stoned him to death. Stephen was the first Christian martyr, killed because of his faith in Jesus.

Acts 7:54-60

After that the lives of the Christians in Jerusalem were in danger, and many of them fled to avoid persecution. But that only helped to spread the message. Instead of being mainly in Jerusalem, Christians were now scattered across the Roman Empire sharing their faith. And they began to share it with people who were not Jews.

Acts 8:26-40

A friend of Stephen's, named Philip, went north to Samaria and won many new followers for Jesus among the Samaritans, who were hated by the Jews because they were not of pure Jewish race. He then went south to Gaza where he met a government official from Ethiopia in East Africa. This man was a 'Godfearer' who was interested in the Jewish faith. He listened to what Philip told him about Jesus, and went back to Ethiopia as a Christian. Philip later travelled north to Caesarea, where he settled and continued his work as a preacher.

Acts 21:8

Acts 9:32-43

Peter, too, travelled from Jerusalem to tell people about Jesus. Many people at Lydda and Joppa joined the church when they saw people whom Peter had healed and heard him preach. Then he was invited to preach to the family of

Acts 10:1-48 — Cornelius, a Roman centurion stationed at Caesarea, who was also a Godfearer.

Cornelius' conversion created a few headaches as well as joys, however. Hitherto most of the Christians had been Jews. Acts 15:1-35 — But if Gentiles were joining the church how should the Jewish Christians behave towards them? Should they eat meals with them or remain segregated? And what was their standing with regard to the old Jewish law? Eventually a meeting of church leaders at Jerusalem decided that non-Jews (usually called Gentiles) should be welcomed, and not burdened with Jewish customs. And later Paul could write of the breaking-down of Galatians 3:28 — racial and cultural barriers through faith in Christ: 'There is neither slave nor free, there is neither male nor female; for you are all one in Christ Jesus.'

Jews and Christians

The first followers of Jesus had no churches where they could worship God. At first those in Jerusalem visited the Jewish temple, and those in other towns continued to worship at the synagogue, just as they had always done. But as time went on orthodox Jews became more hostile to the Christians, and would not allow them to come to the temple or synagogues. And in any case, Christians naturally wanted to meet separately to learn more about Jesus.

So they met in their homes. Christians who owned large houses invited others to join them at least once a week and when possible on the first day of the week, the day the resurrection had taken place. The first Christians in Jerusalem often met at the home of John Mark, for instance, who later wrote Mark's Gospel (Acts 12:12).

Sometimes the meetings took place late at night, when Christians who were slaves had finished their long day's work. Luke actually records an incident when someone fell asleep during a long sermon (Acts 20:7-12). They sang psalms from the Old Testament, or hymns in praise of Jesus which a member of the church had recently composed. There would also be prayers,

and sometimes a reading from the Old Testament. (The New Testament, of course, was not yet written.) And an apostle or some other Christian leader told stories about Jesus and explained his teachings.

The first Christians also often ate meals together. This was a way of showing how much they cared about each other, for the richer ones would share their food with the poor. And during the communal meal they broke some bread and shared it, together with a cup of wine, just as Jesus had done with his disciples at the last supper on the night before his death (Mark 14:22-25). This reminded them of Jesus' death, and they thanked God that Jesus had not only died for them, but was alive again and with them as they worshipped.

The Jewish people were proud of their history and thought of themselves as God's chosen people, different from other nations. They divided people up into the following classes, all of whom are mentioned in the Acts of the Apostles. The class distinction disappeared, of course, when these people became Christians, although the labels continued to be used as convenient descriptions of recognizable groups of people encountered by the apostles.

Jews: people of pure Jewish race, descended from those who lived in the southern kingdom of Judah during Old Testament times.

Gentiles: people belonging to other nations – Greeks and Romans, for example – who had no Jewish ancestors.

Samaritans: people living in the region of Samaria, some of them descended from the members of the northern kingdom of Israel, whom the Assyrians had conquered about 721 BC. They had married foreign people who came to live in their land after the Assyrian conquest, and so they were not of pure Israelite blood. For this reason the Jews of Jesus' day despised them, and some even refused to travel through the district where the Samaritans lived. But Jesus went, and won many followers there (John 4).

Proselytes: non-Jews who believed in the God of the Jews and practised the Jewish way of life. They took part in Jewish worship, kept the Jewish law, and brought up their children as Jews.

Godfearers: other Gentiles who were attracted to the Jewish faith and attended synagogue worship, who were unwilling to obey all the details of the Jewish law. (There were rules, for example, listing what activities were forbidden on the sabbath, and what kind of food Jews were forbidden to eat.)

Paul the traveller

Saul of Tarsus
Acts 8:1

When Stephen was stoned to death for preaching about Jesus, a man named Saul was there, approving of the murder. Yet he was shortly to become one of the most famous Christian evangelists the world has known. He was born of Jewish parents about AD 1 in Tarsus, the main city of the Roman province of Cilicia. His father was a Roman citizen, and this meant that Saul was a Roman citizen too. He had a Roman name – Paul – which he used when he was away from his Jewish home and friends.

The young Saul was sent to school in Jerusalem, where he studied under the famous Rabbi Gamaliel. He joined the party of the Pharisees, and was eager to keep the Jewish law in all its details. He was probably in Jerusalem at the time of Jesus' ministry and death, but there is no record of him having met Jesus then.

When Saul heard Stephen preaching, he was certain of one thing: he hated the followers of Jesus. They were encouraging people to break God's law, he thought. And how could a man who had been crucified like a criminal be God's messiah? The Christians, he decided, must be stamped out before they gained any more influence. So Saul got permission from the high priest to seek out Christians who had fled to Damascus, and to bring them back to Jerusalem for trial.

Acts 9:1-9

He had nearly completed the 140-mile/225-km journey north to Damascus, when something happened which changed his life. He had a vision of Jesus, and heard the voice of Jesus calling him. In a flash he realized that in fighting against the Christians he was really fighting against God himself. He saw that Jesus was God's messiah, and was no longer dead, but alive.

Acts 9:19-25

When he arrived in Damascus he did not arrest the Christians there; instead he began to worship with them. And to everyone's amazement he went to the Jewish synagogues, not to denounce the Christians, but to tell about his new-found faith in Jesus. It was not long before some of the Jews began plotting to kill him, and he escaped by being lowered over the city wall of Damascus in a basket. The persecutor of the Christians was now being persecuted himself.

Acts 9:26-30; Galatians 1:18-24

Three years after he became a Christian, Saul met some of Jesus' followers in Jerusalem. They were afraid of him, thinking that he might be pretending to be a Christian in order to arrest them. But Barnabas befriended Saul and introduced him to some of the apostles, who realized that he was a changed man, and invited him to share their work of preaching in Jerusalem. But once again enemies plotted to kill him, and he had to escape. He then travelled to Caesarea, and sailed from there to his home in Tarsus, where he spent the next ten years, probably preaching and working at the family trade of tent-making. And like Abraham (the founder of the Jewish nation) Saul, who was the founder of many local Christian churches, soon changed his name. For the rest of his life, he was to be known by his Roman name of Paul, which would be more familiar to his non-Jewish audiences.

The first journey, AD 46–47

Acts 11:19-26

Acts 13:1-3

Acts 13:4-12

Antioch in Syria, with a population of about 500,000, was the third largest city in the Roman Empire. It had a thriving church, started not long after Jesus' death by Christians who had fled from Jerusalem because of persecution. And they were the first to welcome non-Jews into the church in large numbers. Barnabas arrived from Jerusalem to investigate what was going on, and was delighted with what he saw. Immediately he went to Tarsus to fetch Saul, and together they taught the new Christians at Antioch for about a year.

But then the church felt the need to send the apostles further afield with their message. So the two set out, taking with them Barnabas' nephew John Mark as assistant. They sailed from Seleucia, the port near Antioch, to the island of Cyprus, which Barnabas, who had been born there, knew well.

They landed at Salamis, where they preached in the Jewish synagogues. They then travelled 100 miles/160km to Paphos, the island's capital. Sergius Paulus, the governor of Cyprus, was so impressed by their preaching that he became a

After his vision of Jesus on the road to Damascus, Saul continued his journey and was taken to a house in Straight Street, seen here through the city's East Gate.

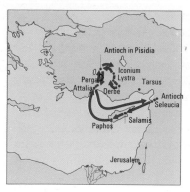

Paul's first journey

Salamis, on the island of Cyprus, was the first stop for Paul and Barnabas. These remains of the gymnasium evoke the powerful Roman civilization which confronted the first-century missionaries.

Christian despite the opposition of a magician who had some influence over him.

From Cyprus the missionaries sailed north to what we now know as Turkey. Although Barnabas was the older of the two, Paul's greater gifts soon made him the leader. They landed near Perga, and went northwards into the mountains, to the Roman province of Galatia. Then John Mark suddenly decided to leave the others and return to Jerusalem. The reasons are unclear; perhaps he was frightened of the dangers the missionaries would face, or just homesick. But in later years he was to prove a valuable leader. When Paul was in prison near the end of his life he referred to Mark in his letters as his friend and fellow-worker. He was probably the author of Mark's Gospel.

Acts 13:13-14

Colossians 4:10; 2 Timothy 4:11; Philemon 24

At Antioch in Pisidia Paul was invited to preach in the Jewish synagogue, and many of the Godfearers became Christians. But the Jews only became jealous and angry when he said that non-Jews need not keep all the details of the Jewish law in order to be acceptable to God. So they drove Paul and Barnabas out of their city.

Acts 13:50

The same thing happened in the next town, Iconium, so Paul and Barnabas fled to Lystra, 25 miles/40km away. There Paul healed a crippled man, and the superstitious locals were so amazed that they thought Paul and Barnabas were the Greek gods Hermes and Zeus in human form. They had some difficulty in explaining that they were messengers of the great God who created the earth.

Acts 14:2

Acts 14:12

Acts 14:19

Then some Jews turned up from Antioch and Iconium, and continued the persecution they had started in their own towns. They stoned Paul till they nearly killed him. But he recovered sufficiently to go on to preach in one more place – Derbe. He and Barnabas then courageously retraced their steps visiting Lystra, Iconium and Antioch again to encourage the new Christians and appoint leaders in the churches. By the time they returned to Antioch in Syria, they had been away for two years, and they had travelled 1,400 miles/2,240km by land and sea.

The second journey, AD 50–52

Acts 15:22-41

Acts 16:1

Acts 16:9-10

The next tour was twice as long. It began some three years later, when Paul decided it was time to go back to the churches he had founded in Galatia. He set off from Antioch, taking a friend named Silas. They went by land through Syria and Cilicia, calling no doubt at Paul's home town of Tarsus. At Derbe, Lystra, Iconium and Pisidian Antioch they found the churches were flourishing. At Lystra they met Timothy, a young Greek friend of Paul's, and took him on their journey.

Paul wanted next to move westwards into the Roman province of Asia and to its great capital city, Ephesus. But circumstances prevented him going there, and Paul and Silas found themselves at Troas, on the north-west coast of Asia Minor. This was the same city as ancient Troy, whose warriors had fought for ten years against the Greeks, 1,200 years before Paul's time.

Here Paul had a dream in which God told him to cross over into Europe and preach there. He and Silas were now joined by Luke, and they took a ship to Neapolis in Greece. From

Paul's second journey

Paul spent eighteen months preaching and teaching in Corinth. The sixth-century BC Temple of Apollo now dominates the site of the ancient city. It is shown here with the fortress of Acro-Corinth in the background.

there they visited cities on the famous Egnatian Way, a Roman road which ran across northern Greece. At Philippi and Thessalonica they established thriving churches, and in the years that followed Paul grew especially fond of the warm-hearted Christians at Philippi. But there was opposition, too. A brief spell in prison ended after an earthquake, and the superstitious town governors released their Christian captives. The missionaries moved on to Berea, but once again Paul was plagued by enemies, this time Jews from Thessalonica. He had to escape quickly and went south to Athens, where he waited for his companions to join him.

Acts 16:19-40

Acts 17:1-15

Acts 17:16-34

Paul had not intended to spend time preaching in Athens. But saddened by the multitude of idols and shrines, he began talking to people about Jesus in the market-place, and challenging the philosophers to discussion. He was asked to explain himself to the city's Council of Elders, who met on a hill known as the Areopagus. When he told them about the resurrection of Jesus some were puzzled, some laughed, but a few believed and became Christians before Paul moved on to Corinth.

Acts 18:1-17

Paul, rejoined by Silas and Timothy, remained in Corinth for eighteen months. The church grew rapidly, even though the moral and social standards of the city were very corrupt. The church was affected by the instability and immorality of the people, and Paul's later letters to the church reveal drunken behaviour during the meetings and wrong relationships among the church members. But several

Paul's third journey

Ephesus was an important seaport on the west coast of Asia Minor (modern Turkey). The theatre there would have been a magnificent sight in Paul's day.

important people became Christians, including a wealthy householder, Titius Justus, in whose house the church met, and Erastus, the city treasurer.

Acts 18:18-23

Eventually Paul and his companions set sail from the port of Cenchreae. They completed the tour with a 1,000-mile/ 1,600-km journey to Antioch by way of Ephesus, Caesarea and Jerusalem. The church was now firmly established not only in Palestine and Asia Minor, but also at important cities in Greece.

Athens was a very religious city. The Acropolis, a flat-topped hill, was the centre of religious life, and the ruins of temples built in the fourth century BC can still be seen there today. This is a reconstruction of what it probably looked like in Paul's time. The large building at the top is the Parthenon, and the tall statue is of Athena, the patron goddess of Athens.

Religions of the Roman Empire

When Paul preached in Athens he began by saying: 'I see that in every way you are very religious.' All over the Roman Empire, religion played an important part in people's lives.

There was the *traditional religion* of the Greeks and Romans, with its myths about Zeus (his Roman name was Jupiter), Apollo, Aphrodite (Venus) and many other gods. By the first century AD many people had ceased to have any real belief in these gods, but they took part in religious ceremonies as a way of showing that they were still loyal to the Roman state and its traditions. The Emperor Augustus tried to revive the old religion, but without much success.

In Augustus' time the practice of *emperor worship* began to develop. The people of the empire were grateful to Augustus for bringing peace after nearly a hundred years of war. They called him 'Saviour of the state'. Especially in the eastern part of his empire – as we learn from coins and inscriptions – he was given titles such as 'saviour', 'son of god' and 'divine father'. He encouraged worship of 'Rome and Augustus'.

The real purpose of this was political rather than religious; it encouraged unity and loyalty among the very varied peoples of the empire. To refuse to take part in the worship of the emperor was a mark of disloyalty, or even of rebellion against the Roman state. Under some later emperors, Christians had to choose whether to deny their belief in Christ by worshipping the emperor, or to risk death by refusing to take part in the ceremonies.

As long as people paid their respects to the emperor in this way, they were free to take part in other religious activities. Many ordinary people were attracted to *magic*, in order to gain power over the evil forces which were

believed to control the world. Paul brought the good news of Jesus to many people involved in magic (Acts 13:6–12; 16:16–18)

Many people, too, believed that their lives were governed by fate. For them *astrology* – studying the movements of the stars – seemed to offer a way of unlocking the secrets of the future, so that the rule of fate need not be so harsh.

And then there were the *mystery religions*. These were secret cults which flooded into the empire mostly from the east. Many of them were based on myths of a goddess whose lover or child was taken from her (usually by death) and later returned to her. They claimed to offer immortality and freedom from guilt. Their worship, practised in great secrecy, would often be dramatic and would work people up to an emotional frenzy. In some of these cults use was made of alcohol, or of psychedelic lighting effects to 'enlarge the consciousness' of the worshippers.

Some of the best-known mystery cults were those of Isis and of Serapis (from Egypt), Cybele (from Asia Minor) and Mithras (from Persia). The Mithras cult was especially popular among Roman soldiers. They took it as far as Hadrian's Wall, in northern England, where a temple of Mithras can still be seen today.

Among educated people *philosophy* sometimes had a greater hold than religion. The influence of Plato (c. 427–348 BC) was still strong. He had argued that the soul is immortal, and that God is one (not many, as in the old Greek myths). But by the first century AD there were also Stoic philosophers, whom Paul met in Athens (Acts 17:18). They taught that men should dutifully accept their fate, because it has been given to them by the principle of Reason which rules the universe. The Epicurean philosophy was

Roman religions did not encourage moral improvement but aimed to protect their adherents from danger and evil. Many gods and goddesses were worshipped, including Jupiter, king of the gods.

Right: Roman emperors were often regarded as divine. Trajan, emperor from AD 98 to 117, was a military genius who conquered Dacia (Romania) for Rome. The empire was at its largest extent when he died.

Below: a Roman sculpture from the early first century AD showing animals being brought for sacrifice at a religious festival.

less severe. Its aim was to achieve happiness through the limited use of pleasure, and to help people to accept the fact that there is no life after death. The Cynic philosophers travelled around teaching anyone who would listen to them on street-corners and in market-places. They questioned the value of many of society's laws and customs. They urged people to live a simple life (their hero was Diogenes, the Athenian famous for having lived in a barrel) and to reject the popular pursuit of affluence.

There were, then, many ways in which people tried to find meaning in life and freedom from their fear of fate and of death. But, then as now, there were also people who looked for happiness without turning to any particular religion or philosophical teaching. Here is the down-to-earth 'philosophy of life' of the Roman poet Martial,

writing about AD 100:
These are the things which
    make life more blessed –
property acquired by birth,
    not by work;
fruitful land, and ever-burning
    hearth;
freedom from lawsuits and
    from having to wear a suit;
a contented mind, a strong and
    healthy body;
friends you can relax with;
simple food, but enough of it;
evenings spent with wine
    enough to take away your
    cares,
but not to get you drunk,
a wife who is plain but brings
    you happiness;
sleep to make the darkness
    short.
Happiness is to be content with
    what you are;
a happy man can contemplate
    the day of death without fear
and without wanting to hasten
    it.

The third journey, AD 52–56

At last Paul was able to fulfil his ambition of visiting Ephesus. A city of 250,000 people, it was famous for its temple of the goddess Artemis (the Romans called her Diana). Craftsmen who worked in silver made fortunes out of modelling and selling little statues of the goddess to people who came for the great annual festival of Artemis.

Acts 19:1-20

Paul spent over two years at Ephesus, preaching for a time in the synagogue, and then in the lecture hall of Tyrannus, which he hired for teaching and discussion. Sick people were healed. Some who practised black magic became Christians and confessed their evil practices, bringing their books of magic spells to be burned in public. The church grew so large and strong that it provoked fierce opposition in the city.

People stopped believing in Artemis, and the silversmiths' trade declined. Fearing that they would go out of business if

Acts 19:23-41

Paul was allowed to continue preaching, a silversmith named Demetrius called a meeting. Full of anger, the craftsmen rushed into the streets. A crowd quickly gathered and followed them to the theatre, dragging along Gaius and Aristarchus, two of Paul's companions. For two hours the theatre – which could hold 25,000 people – was in uproar, as the mob chanted, 'Great is Artemis of the Ephesians!'

At last the town clerk managed to quieten them. He pointed out that the Christians had committed no crime and if anyone had complaints against Paul, he should take it to the normal courts of justice. Unless the crowd went home quickly, he warned, they were in danger of being punished by their Roman rulers for rioting.

The people took his advice and went home. But Paul had to

Paul travelled to Rome in two of the grain ships which regularly sailed the Mediterranean routes. They were designed with a central mast, large square mainsail and small foresail. The oars in the stern acted as rudders.

The man and his methods

Paul was not an impressive man to look at. An early tradition describes him like this: 'A short man, with a bald head and crooked legs; his body is fit and healthy; his eyebrows meet over his nose, which is rather hooked; his face is full of friendliness'. He was able to persuade people to have faith in Jesus. He was a good organizer, too, skilled at founding churches and helping them to keep going under pressure of opposition and disagreement.

Through his Jewish background he knew the Old Testament thoroughly, and he used it frequently in discussion about the Christian faith. And because he was brought up in a Greek city and travelled widely amongst Greek people, he understood their ways of thinking too. He was therefore able to speak about Jesus in a way that would interest the non-Jews to whom he went as a missionary. He spoke Aramaic (the language of Jews in Palestine) and Greek,

so he could go nearly anywhere in the Roman Empire and be easily understood. He once wrote of his desire to 'become all things to all men' in the interest of winning them to the Christian faith (1 Corinthians 9:22).

Being a Roman citizen, he was respected when he travelled around the empire. And on several occasions Paul owed his life to the protection he got from Roman soldiers because of his legal citizenship.

Nothing mattered to Paul more than sharing the good news of Jesus with as many people as he could. He was willing to go through all kinds of suffering and hardship in the course of his work. In his second letter to the Corinthians he lists the dangers he had endured: flogged five times by Jewish authorities, and three times by the Romans; stoned once and shipwrecked on three occasions; he once spent twenty-four hours adrift at sea, and on many occasions was attacked by robbers and people who objected to his

preaching; he was frequently hungry and thirsty, cold and homeless. And he also confesses to the emotional burden of anxiety for the groups he had left behind across the empire (2 Corinthians 11:24-28). He often had to wait months for news of his friends and fellow-workers.

In his missionary work Paul had a plan which he regularly followed. First he started churches in important towns, for example Philippi, Corinth and Ephesus. From there other Christians could travel to smaller towns nearby to start new churches. Then he appointed leaders in each church who would guide the church's worship and care for younger Christians.

He went back to his churches from time to time, to encourage them and to deal with any problems that occurred. But he also kept in touch with them by sending his assistants – men like Titus and Timothy – to visit them, and by writing letters to them. There are thirteen letters written by Paul in the New Testament.

Acts 20:1-6

leave the city, so that the church could grow in peace, and he set off once more for Greece. There had been splits in the church at Corinth, and Paul had sent Titus and had written letters to deal with the troubles. But now he wanted to go there himself. Passing through Philippi, Thessalonica and Berea on the way, he reached Corinth and spent three months there. The troubles in the Corinthian church were put right, and when he heard of yet another Jewish plot to kill him, Paul returned by land to Philippi.

Acts 21:1-15

From there he sailed to Troas, where he was joined by several friends from churches in Greece and Asia Minor. They were taking money from their churches to the poor Christians in Jerusalem. This was Paul's way of showing to the Jewish Christians in Palestine that non-Jewish Christians cared about them, and that they were all part of the one church of Jesus Christ.

Jerusalem to Rome, AD 60–61

Acts 21:27-39

Paul had been in Jerusalem only a few days when he was in trouble again. Hostile Jewish pilgrims – probably visitors from Ephesus – recognized him in the temple. They accused Paul of bringing a non-Jew into the inner court of the temple, where only Jews were allowed. Their report was false, but it quickly caused a riot. Paul was saved from death by soldiers who arrived just in time to remove him to the safety of their barracks in the fortress of Antonia.

Acts 23:16–24:27

For his own safety, Paul was secretly transferred to the provincial governor's headquarters at Caesarea. He was imprisoned there for two years while the governor, Felix, decided what to do with him. When Felix was replaced by Festus, the new governor decided to try Paul in Jerusalem, where his Jewish accusers could state their case. Paul saw little

Acts 25:6-12

hope of getting justice from the Jewish authorities, so he used his right as a Roman citizen and appealed to be tried before the emperor in Rome.

Acts 27:1-44

Paul was put in the charge of a Roman centurion called Julius, who treated him well and allowed his friends Luke and Aristarchus to travel with him. The sea journey to Rome almost ended in disaster, when after two weeks at the mercy of violent storms the ship ran aground on the island of Malta. The cargo of grain had already been thrown overboard to lighten the ship, and the 276 passengers and crew had to swim ashore.

Paul's journey to Rome

Acts 28:1-15

After a three months' stay in Malta, during which time Paul continued to preach about Christ, they sailed again on another grain ship to the Italian port of Puteoli. Paul was allowed to spend a week with Christians there. The last 150 miles/240km to Rome were by road, along the famous Appian Way.

Acts 28:16-30

So Paul came to Rome – an ambition he had long cherished. But he came as a prisoner awaiting trial. A soldier guarded him, but he was allowed to stay in his own private lodgings. There he could write letters to his churches, receive guests, and preach to all who would come to listen. He stayed in these lodgings for two years, and there Luke's narrative ends. We do not know what happened next, but Paul was probably tried before the Emperor Nero and declared innocent. He may well have spent a further two years after that travelling and preaching and encouraging the churches, before finally being martyred for his faith about AD 64 in Rome, when Christians were being picked on and persecuted at a time of social unrest.

For thirty years Paul had obeyed the call which came to him on the Damascus road. He had faced dangers and persecution, shipwreck and opposition. He had planted churches in several provinces of the Roman Empire. He had written the letters which now form a quarter of the New Testament. And shortly before his death he wrote to his friend Timothy: 'I have fought the good fight, I have finished the race, I have kept the faith.' He was the first and greatest 'apostle to the Gentiles'.

2 Timothy 4:7

The seven churches of Asia

The book of Revelation was written – probably around AD 90 – by a Christian named John who had been exiled to the island of Patmos. It is full of visions about the future, written in highly symbolic language. He looks forward to a time when justice will be seen to be done, and God will create a new world in which pain and sorrow, persecution and violence will be no more. In the first three chapters of the book are short letters to seven churches in Asia Minor. They tell something of how Christians were faring towards the end of the first century, mentioning faults and failings as well as strengths and virtues.

Ephesus had a strong church built up by Paul thirty-five years before John wrote (2:1-7). It was one of the major Hellenistic cities of the ancient world.

Smyrna is now the Turkish port of Izmir. A Roman aqueduct which brought water to the town (2:8-11) still remains, as does the Roman forum.

Pergamum was, according to John, 'Satan's throne'. This may refer to the temple of the Greek god Zeus at Pergamum, which was one of the seven wonders of the ancient world (2:12-17). *Thyatira* was well-known for its making of clothes, pottery and brass-work (2:18-29). *Sardis* also was a centre for making and dyeing clothes, hence John's reference to soiled and white garments (3:1-6). *Philadelphia* was the only one of

the seven churches with which John found no fault (3:7-13). *Laodicea* was a wealthy town, whose bankers were known throughout the Roman Empire. In his letter John compares the church with the town's water supply, which was carried by pipes from the hot springs at Hierapolis nearby. The water arrived lukewarm – not hot enough to be soothing and healing, not cold enough to be refreshing (3:14-21).

The remains of ancient Pergamum include this theatre and temple of Dionysus. Emperor worship was first established here.

How the New Testament was compiled

There is little direct evidence of how the New Testament books were collected into a single volume by the early church. It was certainly a gradual process, and it was not until the fourth century that a church Council ratified the list of books already accepted as being unique among many other Christian writings.

Following the Jewish practice, the first Christians regularly read from the Old Testament at their meetings. However, as they were followers of Jesus Christ, it was natural for someone to speak at firsthand about some part of Jesus' life and teaching.

However, as the churches grew in number and the eye-witnesses eventually died, it became necessary to have a written record of these stories. It is likely that a number of people recorded events from Jesus' life, and during the first century AD the four Gospels (Matthew, Mark, Luke and John) were compiled. They had an important place in the life and worship of the early Christians.

Just as the Jews believed that God had uniquely inspired their scriptures, so the first Christians attributed a similar quality to some of their writings. By AD 200 all the churches recognized the four Gospels as the official records of Jesus' life and teaching. Some of Paul's letters to individual churches had also come to be recognized as being necessary to the development of the whole church. It was only later that the remaining books of the New Testament became generally accepted.

The book of Revelation, for instance, was known in the second century but not widely used by Christians until the third. The letter to the Hebrews was not generally recognized as 'scripture' by the churches in the west (Italy and parts of Europe) until the fourth century, partly because of doubts as to whether Paul wrote it.

After some three centuries of discussion, during which most churches had agreed which writings had a unique authority for Christian faith and conduct, the 'canon' or list of accepted books was confirmed by meetings of church leaders. The Council of Laodicea (AD 363) accepted the New Testament as it now stands with the exception of Revelation. In AD 367 a letter from Bishop Athanasius of Alexandria cited a list of books identical to our New Testament, and this list was officially recognized at the Council of Carthage in AD 397.

The early texts

In contrast to the Old Testament, scholars possess thousands of ancient manuscripts of the New Testament. This part of the Bible was originally written down in Greek, but there are also early translations in Latin, Syriac, Egyptian and other languages.

Most of the Greek manuscripts contain a text which became standardized in the fifth century AD. The first printed edition of this Greek text was prepared by the Dutch scholar Erasmus and published in 1516. No questions had been raised as to the accuracy of the standardized text prior to this date. However, several editions published in the sixteenth and seventeenth centuries included notes showing where other manuscripts differed from the standard text of the New Testament. Important examples include the Greek editions of Stephanus, which formed the basis of the King James' Version (or 'Authorized Version') in England (1611), and of Elzevir (1633) which became the standard for European translations.

During the eighteenth and nineteenth centuries, scholars began to investigate the history of the standard text and discovered that many older manuscripts differed in some details from it. It then became more important to establish the age and quality of a manuscript than to be impressed by the number of copies that had survived. Other scholars found that manuscripts could be grouped together in 'families' on the basis of certain shared characteristics, and this resulted in the standard fifth-century text being replaced by older, more accurate texts.

The earliest surviving manuscript of the complete New Testament is *Codex Sinaiticus*, dating from the fourth century. The slightly older *Codex Vaticanus* includes everything up to the ninth chapter of Hebrews. These two manuscripts formed the basis of a Greek text prepared in the nineteenth century. During the last 100 years many fragments of even earlier manuscripts written on papyrus have been discovered. They have enabled scholars to achieve more accurate editions of the New Testament.

Until the fifteenth century when printing was invented in the West, all manuscripts had to be copied by hand. This was usually done by a group of scribes, writing from dictation by a chief scribe. Mistakes inevitably occurred if words were misheard or concentration lapsed. A copyist working on his own could misread the writing from the original manuscript or introduce unintentional errors into the copy. Handwritten manuscripts were too expensive for general use and churches usually owned one which all their members shared.

At first the New Testament books were written on scrolls of papyrus, leather or parchment. But it is thought that from about the second century Christians pioneered the book form ('codex') which we use today.